BPAL
7.15

114 015 1

CHANGED

A114015IN

D1092239

ARNOLD BENNETT
AND H. G. WELLS

THE H. G. WELLS PAPERS
AT THE UNIVERSITY OF ILLINOIS

General Editor: Gordon N. Ray

Henry James and H. G. Wells
Edited by Leon Edel and Gordon N. Ray

Arnold Bennett and H. G. Wells
Edited by Harris Wilson

IN PREPARATION

George Gissing and H. G. Wells
Edited by Royal Gettmann

Bernard Shaw and H. G. Wells
Edited by Gordon N. Ray

ARNOLD BENNETT, *c. 1900*

H. G. WELLS, *1895*

PR
6003
·E6Z54
1960

ARNOLD BENNETT

AND

H. G. WELLS

*A Record of a Personal
and a Literary
Friendship*

Edited with an Introduction by
Harris Wilson

UNIVERSITY OF ILLINOIS PRESS
Urbana, 1960

© Rupert Hart-Davis 1960

Printed in Great Britain by Richard Clay and Company, Ltd.,
Bungay, Suffolk

For
Anna Wilson

CONTENTS

FOREWORD

The correspondence between Arnold Bennett and H. G. Wells extends from 30 September 1897 to 17 February 1931, a few weeks before Bennett's death, and is fullest between 1900 and 1910. From that point the letters tend, with frequent exceptions, toward brevity, and the intervals between letters, again with frequent exceptions, tend to increase. This could be due to several causes. The literary convictions of the two men were largely set by 1910; they had both established themselves among the foremost novelists of their time, and they no longer felt the need to use each other as sounding-boards for their literary theory and practice. Both were prominent and busy literary personalities during the war and after; they lacked the time for an extensive exchange of correspondence. Finally, and perhaps most significantly, the rapid development of transport facilities, especially the motorcar, at the beginning of the century made personal access so much easier that full and detailed correspondence became unnecessary.

I am explicit concerning these possible causes for the relative thinness of the later correspondence because of the danger of misinterpretation. Bennett's biographer, on the basis of testimony from friends of the two men, infers that there was a deterioration in their relationship during the twenties. Wells himself in his treatment of Bennett in

Experiment in Autobiography reveals little personal affection and makes a rather ambiguous statement concerning their later friendship: "We two, he and I, got on in the world abreast—and it was extremely good fun for both of us. Later on we diverged." But even though the progressive sparseness and brevity of the correspondence after 1910 might seem to reinforce these indications of growing coolness, the fact remains that two of the warmest and most affectionate letters Wells wrote to Bennett were in the last year of Bennett's life.

It is fortunate that the correspondence is densest from 1900 to 1910, the most important creative decade for both men in their development as novelists. Their mutual affection allowed a naturalness and candour concerning their work that make the series of letters during this period indispensable for an understanding of their literary method and achievement. The correspondence as a whole provides an illuminating commentary upon the Edwardian and Georgian literary scene. And, most important of all, we see in their letters an intimate reflection of two of the most interesting literary personalities of our century.

In editing the Bennett–Wells correspondence I have striven for as accurate a transcription as print will allow. For the reader's convenience, the style and position of the dates and addresses at the heads of the letters have been standardized, and all names of books, newspapers, etc., have been italicized. For various reasons the names of three ladies have been replaced by initials. For biographical information I have used extensively *The Journals of Arnold Bennett*, edited by Newman Flower (London, 3 vols., 1932–33) and H. G. Wells's *Experiment in Autobiography* (London, 2 vols., 1934). Reginald Pound's *Arnold Bennett* (London, 1952) and Geoffrey West's *H. G. Wells* (London, 1930) have been extremely helpful. But the wealth of material in the H. G. Wells Archive at the University of Illinois Library, Urbana, Illinois, has been my chief resource.

There is a good balance in the letters—eighty-six from Bennett to Wells, eighty-seven from Wells to Bennett. To my knowledge, these comprise all the surviving correspondence between the two men except a few un-dated notes which I have excluded on the grounds of brevity and lack of significance or interest. I have included thirty-three letters from Bennett to Mrs Wells, a great many of which deal directly with Wells's work, two letters from Mrs Marguerite Bennett, a short article concerning Wells by Bennett, and a letter from Bennett's secretary. Of the letters in this edition, Pound and West have printed in their biographies twenty-three letters (mostly short passages thereof) from Wells to Bennett; Pound has printed sixteen letters from Bennett to Wells and one from Bennett to Mrs Wells. The remaining 170 letters are published here for the first time. I have appended a number of surrounding documents which have critical or biographical relevance to the correspondence. The first volume of this series of publications from the Wells Archive, *Henry James and H. G. Wells*, provides valuable supplementary material, especially Wells's "The Contemporary Novel" and James's "The Younger Generation."

My major debt is to Dr Gordon N. Ray, Vice-President and Provost of the University of Illinois, and General Editor of the H. G. Wells papers, through whose good offices I was permitted the pleasant and absorbing task of this edition. I am indebted to Mr George Lazarus for photostats of Wells's letters to Bennett and for lending the originals for checking, to the Public Trustee for permission to print Bennett's letters, and to Mrs Marguerite Bennett and Miss Winifred Nerney for permission to print their letters. In am grateful to Miss Eva Faye Benton and Mr T. E. Ratcliffe of the University of Illinois Library Staff, and Professor Bruce Harkness of the University of Illinois English Department, for friendly and competent aid on various details. Mr Rupert Hart-Davis has gone far beyond the normal call of editorial duty in his contribution. Mrs Charles H. Shattuck's detailed knowledge of the Wells Archive has brought her very close to the status of collaborator in this edition, although such errors as remain are my sole responsibility.

INTRODUCTION

On 30 September 1897 Enoch Arnold Bennett, a thirty-year-old editor of a penny magazine for women, wrote a brief letter of appreciation to Herbert George Wells, a thirty-one-year-old author of scientific romances, who had already been hailed by W. T. Stead in his *Review of Reviews* as "a man of genius." Wells answered Bennett with cordiality and at some length. Thus began a personal and literary friendship that was to continue unbroken for a third of a century.

At the time he wrote to Wells, Bennett could make little claim to distinction in letters. He had arrived in London in 1889, a very provincial young man from the north, as a shorthand clerk in a law office. The efficiency that was to become a legend in later years brought him quick if modest success as a clerk, but the widening of his intellectual and cultural horizons, largely through his friendship with Frederick Marriott, soon made the life of the law office impossible for him. He gained a taste of the material rewards of writing from a parody of Grant Allen's *What's Bred in the Bone* published in *Tit-Bits*, for which he received twenty guineas, and offered proof of his artistic capacity in a short story, "A Letter Home," which was accepted by the *Yellow Book*. In the meantime he had begun his first novel and terminated his career as a clerk. With the aid of a £300 loan from his father

Bennett bought shares in and became assistant editor of *Woman* in 1894. By 1896 he had become editor and also attained a small reputation as a reviewer in Lewis Hind's the *Academy*. In 1897 he completed his novel, *A Man from the North*, which was not published until the following year. At the time of his first letter to Wells, Bennett was still at the threshold of one of the most extraordinarily successful careers in English literary history.

Wells's career, on the other hand, was already under way. He had settled in London for a second time in 1888 in ill health and with five pounds in his pocket. He supported himself first as an assistant master at Henley House School and then as a tutor in the London Tutorial College of the University Correspondence College, during which time he received his B.Sc. degree from London University with first-class honours in zoology and second-class honours in geology. This academic success enabled him to marry in 1891. But the pedagogical career to which he was apparently committed ended in physical collapse. Forced to live by his pen, he achieved a minor success with informal essays in Harry Cust's *Pall Mall Gazette* and short stories in Hind's *Pall Mall Budget*. And his real accession to literary prominence and fortune came in 1895, when *The Time Machine* appeared serially in W. E. Henley's *New Review*; and the book, issued in July of the same year, marked Wells as a "coming man," as an article in the August *Bookman* attests. *The Island of Dr. Moreau* and *The Wheels of Chance* in 1896 further enhanced his reputation; at the end of the year Wells could record with satisfaction that he had earned £1056. 7s. 9d. By the time he received Bennett's first letter Wells was, in his own phrase, "fairly launched at last."

That Bennett and Wells would form a personal friendship was almost inevitable. Wells writes in his autobiography: "We were both about of an age; to be exact he was six months younger than I; we were both hard workers, both pushing up by way of writing from lower middle-class surroundings, where we had little prospect of anything but a restricted salaried life, and we found we were pushing with quite surprising ease; we were learning much the same business, tackling much the same obstacles, encountering similar prejudices and antagonisms and facing similar social occasions. We both had a natural zest for life and we both came out of a good old English radical tradition. We were liberal, sceptical and republican."

Yet there were important differences in background. Bennett's father was admitted as a solicitor in 1876. Until that time, during Arnold's first ten years of life, the family's social and economic status had been certainly that of the lower middle-class—the father's occupations being in sequence unsuccessful potter, draper, and pawnbroker; the family's residence shifting from one more or less poverty-stricken section of Burslem to another. But in 1878 the Bennetts moved to a respectable address in Waterloo Road, and two years later the elder Bennett was able to build his own house in Waterloo Road between Hanley and Burslem and to consider himself rightly a respected and successful citizen. From the time he was twelve or thirteen until his departure for London at twenty-one, Arnold Bennett's environment, compared with Wells's, was well-ordered and prosperous.

Wells, like Bennett, spent his early years as the son of a shopkeeper. But Wells's father, Joseph, unlike Bennett's, was far from being a man on the rise. He subordinated his vocation as the proprietor of a small china and glassware shop to his avocation as a cricketer; in fact, it was the sale of cricket supplies in addition to crockery and china that provided the family with a meagre subsistence. But a broken leg in 1877 ended Joseph Wells's career as a professional cricketer and seriously diminished the family income. In 1880, not long after the Bennetts moved into their own home in Waterloo Road, the Wells family broke asunder. The mother went into service as a housekeeper at Uppark in Sussex; the father remained in ineffectual charge of the china shop at Bromley; the thirteen-year-old H. G. went to Windsor for his first trial as a draper's apprentice. From that time H. G. Wells was, except for occasional periods with his mother at Uppark, on his own. One has only to read his autobiography to know what he endured and what he overcame— poverty, social and intellectual degradation, ill-health. When he arrived in London at twenty-one, Wells was already a cynical, resourceful man of the world.

Bennett at his majority knew a world that was grimly materialistic, deadly hostile to the spirit of art. He left it with no qualms. But it was also a world in which hard work and steady purpose had their rewards. "Self-help" was a demonstrable reality in Burslem, and his lifelong conviction of that reality made Bennett in many ways one of the last Victorians. Edwin Clayhanger's thoroughly middle-class life falls far short of its ideal, but nevertheless it is useful and rewarding as lives go, and Bennett views it with sympathy. Wells knew a world in which pure accident of birth, health, or circumstance could thwart and crush any individual, no matter what his potentiality; and he could easily recall times when only happy accident, or what he termed "lucky moments," intervened to save him from the fate that haunted Kipps—that drain pipe in which draper's shopmen crawled until they died.

This basic difference in experience and viewpoint was bound to emerge as Wells's and Bennett's friendship matured. They must have spent many hours in conversation defining and perhaps, at least on Bennett's part, trying to reconcile their views. The disagreement is best reflected in the series of letters in 1905. In February Bennett replies to a missing letter from Wells, in which Wells had apparently chided him for expressing a somewhat naïve admiration for fine hotels. Bennett protests that Wells has missed the irony. In April Bennett in turn objects to Wells's attack, in *A Modern Utopia*, on the Hampstead middle-class. He accuses Wells of revealing his class-prejudice and displaying a complete lack of social perspective. Wells retaliates in a letter concerning Bennett's novel, *Sacred and Profane Love*. He charges Bennett with a preoccupation with "surface values," an inability to penetrate beneath the superficial. Bennett answers directly, in one of the most candid passages he ever wrote, that Wells's charges are essentially true, but that Wells himself, in being a "passion for justice incarnate," had his own limitations: "You won't have anything to do with 'surface values' at all. You don't merely put them in a minor place; you reject them. . . . You will never see it, but in rejecting surface values you are wrong. As a fact they are just as important as other values. But reformers can't perceive this."

Considering this divergence in outlook, one wonders how the personal friendship between the two men survived Wells's spasms of truculence that alienated so many friends much closer in thought than Bennett. But friends they remained. As Wells writes in his autobiography, "After his first visit to Sandgate [in August 1900], we never lost touch with each other. We never quarrelled, we never let our very lively resolve to 'get on' betray our mutual generosity." The reasons for the consistently amicable relationship between the two men lie in their personalities and characters.

Wells was an intensely attractive man when he chose to be. A great deal of testimony exists to his magnanimity and graciousness as a host, his charm and intellectual appeal as a conversationalist; his letters to Bennett contain many examples of the warm and affectionate humour that makes comparisons of the early Wells and Dickens so common. Bennett records in a *Journal* entry of 31 July 1904: "Nearly all Wells's conversation would make good table-talk and one has a notion that it ought not to be wasted; it is so full of ideas and of intellectual radicalism. It seems a pity that it should not be gathered up. But after all there is a constant supply of it. You might as well be afraid of wasting the water from a brook." To Bennett, with his stammer and reserve, Wells's articulateness and liveliness were things to be envied and, above all, cherished. And Bennett, with his wisdom, his ability to see a person whole and to discount faults, cherished his relationship with Wells enough to be certain that Wells's intermittent pugnacity did not destroy it.

Bennett also had a tremendous respect for Wells's mind. He undoubtedly considered him a genius both as a novelist and as a social philosopher. Early in the correspondence Bennett writes, "No one knows more about the *craft* of fiction than you do," and, more than half seriously, that it was his ambition "after 25 years of study, meditation and prayer, to attempt an elaborate monograph on you and let this be the climax of my career." As late as 1926, long after Wells's novels had taken a direction with which Bennett could not have sympathized, Bennett writes concerning *William Clissold*: "This is an *original* novel. My novels never are." And *The Outline of*

B

History "staggered" Bennett. He wrote Mrs Wells in 1920, "I cannot get over it. It's a life work." In 1929, in an article for the *Realist*, Bennett states: "No imaginative author of modern times has exerted an influence equal to that of Wells."

There was, in fact, a deep mutual respect between the two men. In 1912 Wells wrote to Bennett "You have the best mind in Europe (in many respects)" and in 1924, "You are the master craftsman. There is no one like you." Wells also felt strongly in Bennett the generosity of spirit that endeared him to everyone who knew him well. But from beginning to end, and with Bennett's calculated sufferance, Wells dominated the friendship. When Wells visited Bennett at Trinity Hall Farm in December 1902, Bennett's mother and sister, according to Pound, re-sented Wells's condescension to Bennett and wondered how he bore it. Even when Wells, in a fit of impatience, threw a pillow at Bennett, he did not retaliate. Through-out the first fifteen years of their correspondence, Bennett wrote long, detailed critiques of Wells's books, but Wells's appraisals, even of *The Old Wives' Tale*, which he recognized immediately as a great novel, were brief, though usually, it is true, penetrating. It is particularly revealing to note Bennett's long, painstaking comment-aries on such books as *A Modern Utopia* and *Mankind in the Making*, which could not possibly have held great interest for him. As late as 1920 we find Bennett proof-reading a reprint of *The Outline of History*, and within a year of his death Bennett wrote a long, carefully reasoned defence of Wells, who had embroiled himself, to the consternation of his friends and admirers, in a futile and almost hysterical quarrel with a former collaborator and the Authors' Society.

Wells's statement in his autobiography concerning Bennett contains some truth: "He was impermeable. He learnt with extraordinary rapidity and precision. He was full of skills and information. The bright clear mosaic of impressions was continually being added to and all the pieces stayed in their places. He did not feel the need for a philosophy or for a faith or for anything to hold them together." But this estimate shows how much of Bennett Wells missed, how much he was temperamentally incapable of finding out. Bennett, like James and Galsworthy, had a deep feeling for the quality in human existence that Yeats was describing when he asked:

> How but in custom and in ceremony
> Are innocence and beauty born?

And yet, when Wells wrote in 1906, "Incidentally, I want to make you a Socialist," Bennett could reply with perfect sincerity, "You will find it impossible to make me a socialist, as I already am one." Wells mistook Bennett's breadth of viewpoint for shallowness, as so many others have done during and since his time. Bennett's apparent preoccupation with "surface values" was not the result of an impecunious and drab adolescence for which he was

eternally trying to compensate. Bennett viewed life very
coolly and objectively, and his conclusions concerning it
—that the trappings had, in their own way, as much
significance as the more immanent aspects—were logic-
ally defensible and perhaps more "scientific" in terms of
human nature than Wells's own conclusions. Bennett
asks Wells in a letter concerning *Kipps*: "Why this immense animus against the 'nace' class of person, since we
are all human together? Am I to understand that in your
opinion as a purposeful observer of life the 'nace' class is
more ridiculous, or less worthy of sympathy, or less the
outcome of natural and inevitable causes, than any other
class?" But after 1905 Bennett did not press his case.
And the measure of his affection and forebearance is
Wells's statement, less than six months before Bennett's
death, "Arnold . . . you are the best friend I've ever had."

"Bennett—Wells—who else is there?" Wells wrote
Bennett in July 1909, a puzzling statement to those who
have formed their literary tastes since 1930. Of the
novelists writing in the reign of Edward VII, only Conrad, James, and Forster, all of restricted popularity at the
time, have retained the substantial respect of critics. But
in 1909, with *The Old Wives' Tale* and *Tono-Bungay*
recognized contemporary masterpieces among the dis-
criminating, Bennett and Wells, both just turned forty,
were established among the leading novelists of their
time.

The correspondence between them is a valuable statement of their literary conviction and practice, especially in the years before World War I, before Wells was completely absorbed by his dream of the New Republic and the Open Conspiracy, and before Bennett became a kind of journalistic ambassador of the arts. Wells, after *Mr. Britling Sees It Through* in 1916, left the "literary" novel almost entirely behind him, and although art may be propaganda, as George Orwell maintains, Wells made most of his later novels bear too heavy a load. Bennett, except for that strange anomaly, *Riceyman Steps*, can probably make little claim to permanent literary distinction after *These Twain* in 1916, although some see in *Lord Raingo*, and even in *The Pretty Lady*, a prolongation of power.

Bennett's position with regard to Wells's literary method is in some respects the same as James's and Conrad's. Again and again he pleads with Wells to be more careful with details. In *Anticipations* Bennett notes a number of passages displaying a turgidity or "confusedness" that could have been eliminated by careful revision. Concerning *Mankind in the Making* Bennett comments even more vehemently and specifically about overloaded sentences, badly-arranged words, bad grammar, faulty punctuation, inelegancies of one sort or another. Finally, in a letter about *Kipps*, he writes reproachfully, "You said last year, you even faithfully promised that you were going to write with more care. God-a-mercy! After the sentence on p. 409 beginning: 'Next to starting a haberdasher's shop,' I renounce the crusade. I respectfully give you up. Damn it, after all it doesn't matter how you write." But Bennett didn't give him up, at least for well over a decade. His proof-reading for Wells was undoubtedly motivated by his benevolent desire to impose his own passion for meticulousness upon Wells's style. Bennett makes one final attempt to persuade Wells to better ways. In a letter to Mrs Wells concerning *The Outline of History* he exhorts her to try to do something about the mechanics of her husband's composition. He writes rather wistfully, "I don't care to seem to be always insisting to H. G. about details. I have no exaggerated idea of their importance, and I can keep the perspective as well as most folks. But these details *have* importance, and someone ought to see to them." As a reward for his pains Bennett did the proof-reading, or at least a part of it, for the one-volume reprint of *The Outline of History*.

Bennett's admonitions had little, if any, effect on Wells. He remained unregenerate to the end. He writes defiantly to Bennett, with deliberate misspellings: "The stile of my general design, the stile of my thought—C'est moi." His justification is best stated in a letter to Bennett in 1904 in which he writes, "except among passages of high value I don't see the force of writing for beauty of phrase." Again, in his autobiography he answers a question from Conrad asking him whether a boat "sat or rode or danced or quivered on the water?" "I said that in nineteen cases out of twenty I would just let the boat be there in the commonest phrases possible." Wells's manuscripts of his novels are extensively revised in places, but in general they bear out his admission that "the larger part of my fiction was written lightly and with a certain haste." Yet he was capable, as he claims, of evocative phrase: for instance, in an episode in *Tono-Bungay* Beatrice rides on horseback directly in the path of George Ponderevo in his experimental aircraft. He soars over her by a narrow margin, and when he returns after landing: "'Those great wings,' she said, and that was all."

In his own way Bennett was as dedicated to the novel as an art-form as was James, at least in his early development. He was profoundly influenced in his serious work by George Moore and the French realists and was much given to theories of fiction derived from them. This led to a strong reaction from Wells and drew from him an explicit statement of his own literary theory: "In so far as any man's work squares with the standards of any other man's work it doesn't count. All fairly good work has its excellence in something which is not commensurable with anything outside itself. . . . For my own part I am a purblind laborious intelligence exploring that cell of Being called Wells." Much of the early correspondence is concerned with literary method, especially characterization. Wells feels in Bennett's characters little of the vividness or credibility of characters like Becky Sharp; he suggests that Bennett could have heightened the individuality of one of the characters in *Anna of the Five Towns* by adding a little touch of vanity about the shape of his nose. Bennett replies that Wells is antediluvian in his conception of characterization, that instead of Becky Sharp he should take as standards Eugénie Grandet, Madame Bovary or Maisie. "Have you grasped the fact that what I aim at is the expression of general moods, whether of a person or a whole scene, a constant synthetising of emotion, before the elucidation of minor parts of character?"

Both men are discerning, candid critics of each other's work. Wells saw very early the flaw in Bennett that was to prevent him, except in one or two novels, from attaining the first rank. Concerning *Anna of the Five Towns* Wells wrote, "Gissing, Moore and the impersonal school and a certain consciousness of good intentions are evident. . . . My impression [is] that of a photograph a little under-developed." This "consciousness of good intentions" is in all Bennett's serious novels; he is so evidently working for objective, unsentimentalized effects that spontaneity and vividness of characterization tend to disappear. Few memorable characters emerge from Bennett's serious novels. Edwin Clayhanger, Hilda Lessways, Lord Raingo are individualities, it is true, but the reader asks with Henry James, "Yes, yes, but is this *all*?" Few characters have been subjected to such objective, detailed scrutiny, but they lack the appeal of universality; they come to mind as case-studies in a sociology text. It is this almost universal drabness that has prompted many critics to wish that Bennett had transferred some of the verve of his "fantasias" and "frolics" to his serious work, but such a wish indicates a lack of serious examination of even the best of the lighter fiction, which is artistically irresponsible. As Wells comments, "the clever Bennett is going to be a fearful job for the artist Bennett to elude." One of Bennett's main defects as a novelist is that in most of his serious work he seems to stand too much in awe of what he is trying to do and never loses the "consciousness of good intentions" that Wells warned him against.

Bennett saw just as clearly Wells's chief liability as a novelist. It is startling to read Bennett's charge in 1905: "You always recur to a variation of the same type of hero, and you always will, because your curiosity about individualities won't lead you further ... Art, really, you hate ... and the mischief is that, though you will undoubtedly do a vast amount of good in the world, you will get worse and worse, more and more specialised, more and more scornful." Wells's career followed essentially the line that Bennett foresaw. Very early, in 1902, Wells wrote to Bennett, "There is something other than either story writing or artistic merit which has emerged through the series of my books, something one might regard as a new system of ideas—'thought'." His later novels subjugate the "story writing or artistic merit" more and more to the idea. It is labouring the obvious to say that after 1916 Wells resolutely turned his back upon the novel as an art form. His dedication to "ecology" and his willingness to use the novel as a vehicle to give his social theories wider circulation and more general acceptance were in his own mind completely justifiable, and it is not in the scope of this introduction to judge the ultimate wisdom of his decision. Henry James qualifies his reservations concerning *Marriage* with the statement: "Mind you that the restriction I may seem to you to lay on my view of your work, still leaves that work more convulsed with life and more brimming with blood than any it is given me nowadays to meet." One may be permitted regret that the gifts displayed in the early novels should have been so deliberately cast aside.

The differences between Bennett and Wells in their literary conviction and practice should not, however, be over-emphasized. Essentially those differences are superficial. It is significant that Wells, in his *Experiment in Autobiography*, does not classify Bennett with James and Conrad as being representative of the purely artistic approach. A close examination of their statements about each other's work reveals that their objections are concerned primarily with tone and attitude, not with subject-matter or, except in the comparatively superficial sense already discussed, method.

In "Fallow Fields of Fiction," an article published in the *Academy* in 1901, Bennett anticipates Wells's later, and much better known, "The Contemporary Novel" of 1911. Bennett here deplores the conventional restriction of the novel to five major types: the domestic, historical, criminal, theological, and bellicose—all centring around "two men and a maid." He pleads for novels dealing with railway organization, local politics, and all other aspects of contemporary human activity. In an *English Review* article of 1913, "The Story Teller's Craft," Bennett confesses, "yet I am obliged to say that, as the years pass, I attach less and less importance to good technique in fiction. I love it, and I have fought for a better recognition of its importance in England, but I now have to admit that the modern history of fiction will not support me." And he warns the writer against "Stylites" and "sub-Flauberts" who would try to impose artificial restrictions upon fiction.

Wells urges the same expansion of subject-matter in "The Contemporary Novel": "We are going to write about it all. We are going to write about business and finance and politics and precedence and pretentiousness and decorum and indecorum, until a thousand pretences and ten thousand impostures shrivel in the cold, clear air of our elucidations." Wells discerns two movements in contemporary fiction: a native tendency toward discursiveness and variety, and a tendency, springing largely from the French realists, toward exhaustiveness and amplitude. He cites as the two best examples of these tendencies *The Old Wives' Tale*, representing the native "discursive" movement, and *Clayhanger*, the foreign "exhaustive" movement. And Wells, like Bennett, scorns the "adjudicators" and their attempts to formalize and restrict the novel.

Henry James, in "The New Novel" (1914), saw clearly the close resemblance between the literary practice of Bennett and Wells. He places both in the new school of "saturation," although he makes an accurate distinction when he designates Wells's method as essentially "extensive" as opposed to the "intensive" saturation of Bennett. The main contribution of Bennett and Wells, and the Edwardian novelists in general, to the English novel was the broadening and intensification of the treatment of subject-matter. Their literary method remains essentially Victorian. The leisurely and minute exposition of character, situation, and scene represents no advance over Thackeray and Dickens, and it is this quality in the work of Bennett, Wells and Galsworthy that excited the animosity of Virginia Woolf and makes many of their novels such heavy going for most readers today. Wells portrayed in *Ann Veronica* one of the very first women in English fiction frankly to feel sexual desire. The novel created a great public protest and gained Wells a host of fervent young disciples among both sexes. Bennett in *The Pretty Lady* wrote a novel about a prostitute, which was threatened with censorship, and became one of his best-selling novels. But today, with such subject-matter a commonplace, the reader is hard pressed to find permanent distinction in either book.

The fact of the matter is that to both men literature in the belletristic sense was essentially an avocation. Late in his life Bennett wrote: "I have not had a clear and fixed ambition. I began to write novels because my friends said I could. The same for plays. But I always had a strong feeling for journalism, which feeling is as strong as ever it was," and Wells revolted against Conrad, Hueffer, and James with the statement, "I am a journalist. . . I refuse to play the 'artist.' If sometimes I am an artist it is a freak of the gods. I am a journalist all the time and what I write *goes now*—and will presently die."

To understand the prodigious, uneven production of Wells and Bennett, one must understand their age. They came upon the literary scene at a propitious time for young men desiring a career in letters. The Education Act of 1870 was just beginning to have its full effect. During 1870 the number of new novels published in England was 381; during 1900 the number of "juvenile works, novels, tales and other fiction" had increased to 2109. Harmsworth, with the massive circulation of *Tit-Bits*, *Answers* and the *Daily Mail*, had demonstrated the lucrative market for sensational newspapers; and periodicals were springing up almost daily. Both Bennett and Wells began their careers, not as serious, dedicated literary artists, but as contributors to this journalistic ephemera.

It was an age, also, of great optimism, almost, in comparison with the 1890's, of ebullience on the part of intellectuals. The relationship between literary men and statesmen is reminiscent of the eighteenth century. John Galsworthy and Winston Churchill worked hand in hand to institute prison reform, the one through his play, *Justice*, the other through his position as Home Secretary. A dinner given by Beatrice and Sidney Webb included Wells, G. B. Shaw and the future Liberal prime minister, Asquith. G. K. Chesterton looked back on his youth when "A cloud was on the mind of men, and wailing went the weather," and rejoiced that he had lived to see "God and the good Republic come riding back in arms." Winston Churchill remembers the period as one when "statesmen, writers, philosophers, scientists, poets, all moved forward in hope and buoyancy, in sure confidence that much was well, and that all would be better."

Both Wells and Bennett, as they gained literary stature, became intensely involved in the events and the spirit of their time. Wells, through the Fabians, through his position, after *Anticipations*, as unofficial prophet for Western civilization, conceived his principal mission to be a manipulator of men and cultures through ideas, and scorned "the artist living angrily in a stuffy little corner of pure technique." Bennett was never to lose completely his dedication to the novel as an art form—it was to have a late revival in *Riceyman Steps* in 1923—but his important government post during the war, the prominence and influence of his book page in the *Evening Standard* in the twenties, and above all the strong hedonistic element in his character that responded so avidly to the hedonism that was in many ways one of the most salient characteristics of the Edwardian and

Georgian periods—all these prevented the concentration necessary for him to become the novelist he might have been.

One of the most appealing aspects of the correspondence between Bennett and Wells is the record it provides of the ideas and activities of two literary men completely engaged with their world. Even if one feels that this engagement was at the sacrifice of their literary achievement—as the great weight of present critical opinion suggests—it still remains refreshing in the face of the negativism or passivity of most English and American novelists since their time. The reader of the correspondence finds it particularly fitting that Wells should write in the last year of Bennett's life, "What a good friendship it has been!" The two of them moved together from very low beginnings to eminence, and they made their way by their own talents, by a labour that is beyond the compass of most human beings. And through it all they remained men of infinite good will. It is doubtful whether we shall see their like again.

HARRIS WILSON

University of Illinois
  February, 1960

I

BENNETT TO WELLS

6 *Victoria Grove*[1]

30 *September* 1897   *Chelsea S. W.*

DEAR SIR,

For a long time I have been intending to write to you, and express my appreciation of your work, and also to ask what is your connection with Burslem and the potteries. Burslem (where I come from) is mentioned at the beginning of *The Time Machine*,[2] and one of your short stories runs over the entire pottery district—I forget the title of it.[3]

I enclose my review of your last book.[4]

Believe me, dear Sir,

Faithfully yours

E. A. BENNETT

(editor of *Woman*) [5]

[1] The home of Frederick Marriott, art master at Goldsmiths' College, London, where Bennett had been a paying guest since the spring of 1891. The Marriotts and their friends, intellectual and cultured, were an important influence in Bennett's life.

[2] 1895.

[3] "The Cone," first published in *Unicorn*, 18 September 1895, reprinted as the tenth story in *The Plattner Story and Others*, 1897. "The Cone" concerns the vengeance of Horrocks, manager of a blast furnace company in the pottery district, upon Raut, an outsider who has formed a liaison with Horrocks's wife. One night Horrocks takes Raut, ostensibly on an inspection tour, to a ramp above the furnaces, and pushes him into one of the chimneys. Raut

2

WELLS TO BENNETT

Heatherlea [1]
Worcester Park

[*October* 1897]   *Surrey*

DEAR SIR,

Oddly enough I had just overcome a strong impulse to write and thank you for your notice in *Woman*, when your letter arrived. As a reviewer, I learnt long ago the suspicious quality of such gratitude. But now you have given me the chance let me thank you very warmly for the support you have always given me.

You raise the point of the transparent eyelids in your review,[2] but there is another difficulty behind that which really makes the whole story impossible. I believe it to be insurmountable. Any alteration of the refractive index of the eye lenses would make vision impossible. Without such alteration the eyes would be visible as glassy globules. And for vision it is also necessary that there

---

[1] Wells and his second wife, Amy Catherine (Jane), had moved to Worcester Park from Lynton, Maybury Road, Woking, in late 1896.   [2] See Appendix A, p. 258.

---

lives a few agonized moments by clinging to a cone which regulates the heat from the furnace, but soon burns to death.

[4] *The Invisible Man*, 1897.

[5] A penny weekly, founded in 1890, addressed to the growing audience of women readers.

should be visual purple behind the retina and an opaque cornea and iris. On these lines you would get a very effective short story but nothing more.

About Burslem—I'm not a native. But years ago I spent two or three months at Etruria and the district made an immense impression on me. I wish I knew the people. I felt dimly then and rather less dimly today vast possibilities there. Think of Trentham, white Newcastle, and that Burslem Hanley ridge jostling one another—the difference in the lives and "circles of thought" there must be! And I've sat in 'Trury woods in the springtime, bluebells all about me, and seen overhead the smoke from Granville's (I think it's Granville's) Iron Works streaming by under the white clouds.[1] But I don't know the people and "cram" is vile. I shall never do it.

Yours very faithfully

H. G. WELLS

[1] In the spring of 1888, after more than six months of invalidism caused by a crushed kidney and a lung affliction, Wells visited William Burton, a college friend, and his wife in their home at Etruria. One afternoon toward the end of his visit, as he recalls in his *Experiment in Autobiography*, "I went out by myself to a little patch of surviving woodland amidst the industrialized country, called 'Trury Woods.' There had been a great outbreak of wild hyacinths that year and I lay down among them to think. It was one of those sun-drenched afternoons that are turgid with vitality. Those hyacinths in their upright multitude were braver than an army with banners and more inspiring than trumpets.

"'I have been dying for nearly two-thirds of a year,' I said, 'and I have died enough.'

"I stopped dying then and there, and in spite of moments of some provocation I have never died since." (I, 310.)

3

BENNETT TO WELLS

10 *October* 1897   6 *Victoria Grove S.W.*

MY DEAR SIR,

I am very glad to have your letter, and very glad to find that the Potteries made such an impression on you. I lived there till I was 21, and have been away from it 9 years, and only during the last few years have I begun to see its possibilities. Particularly this year I have [been] deeply impressed by it. It seems to me that there are immense possibilities in the very romance of manufacture—not wonders of machinery and that sort of stuff—but in the tremendous altercation with nature that is continually going on—and in various other matters. Anyhow I am trying to shove the notions into my next novel.[1] Only it wants doing on a Zolaesque scale. I would send you a rough sketch of my somewhat vague ideas in this direction, but fear to bore you. To my mind it is just your field. As for the people, I know 'em inside out, and if you are a Northern man you would grasp them instinctively.

I am quite sure there is an aspect of these industrial districts which is really *grandiose*, full of dark splendours, and which has been absolutely missed by all novelists up

----

[1] To be published as *Anna of the Five Towns* in 1902.

to date. Tirebuck [1] in *Miss Grace of All Souls* was too much interested in his individual characters to note synthetically the general aspect, and Nevinson[2] in *Valley of Tophet* also let it escape him.

I trouble you with all this because you are the first man I have come across whom the Potteries has impressed, emotionally. There are a number of good men in the Potteries, but I have never yet met one who could be got to see what I saw; they were all inclined to scoff.

Sincerely yours
E. A. BENNETT

4

WELLS TO BENNETT

Heatherlea

[*December* 1897]   Worcester Park

MY DEAR BENNETT,

(If I may leap a gulf in intercourse and drop the 'Dear Sir') I have just come upon your last letter again, about the Potteries and am moved by your phrase "altercation with nature" to ask if you have discovered the magni-

---

[1] William Edwards Tirebuck, a Welsh novelist (d. 1900). *Miss Grace of All Souls*, 1895, concerns the rigours of life in a small coal-mining town.

[2] Henry Woodd Nevinson (1856–1941). *The Valley of Tophet*, 1896, is a collection of twelve short stories of life in a coal-mining district.

ficent Conrad yet? If not, read *Almayer's Folly* and *The
Outcast of the Islands*.[1] It's thick in places and he ham-
mers in and repeats but *it's the palette*.

Yours very faithfully

H. G. WELLS

5

BENNETT TO WELLS

8 *December* 1897   6 *Victoria Grove S.W.*
MY DEAR WELLS,

I owe you a good turn for pointing out Conrad to me.
I remember I got his first book, *Almayer's Folly*, to review with a batch of others from Unwin, and feeling at
the time rather bored (*you* know the feeling—I get
through 50 or 60 novels a month for two papers) I
simply didn't read it at all—wrote a vague and discreet
par. and left it.

I have just read his new book *The Nigger of the Narcissus*,[2] which has moved me to enthusiasm. Where did
the man pick up that style, and that *synthetic* way of

[1] Wells, in the *Saturday Review*, 16 May 1896, had written: "*An
Outcast of the Islands* is perhaps the finest piece of fiction that has
been published this year, as *Almayer's Folly* was one of the finest
published in 1895."

[2] Bennett wrote in his *Journal*, 6 December 1897: "This afternoon, reading in *New Review* . . . the conclusion of Joseph Conrad's
superb book, *The Nigger of the Narcissus*, I had a mind to go on at
once with my Staffordshire novel, treating it in the Conrad manner,
which after all is my own, on a grander scale." (I, 64.)

UNIVERSITY OF WINNIPEG

Winnipeg,   2E9

DISCARDED

gathering up a general impression and flinging it at you? Not only his style, but his attitude, affected me deeply. He is so consciously an artist. Now Kipling isn't an artist a bit. Kipling doesn't know what art is—I mean the art of words; *il ne se préoccupe que de la chose racontée.*[1] He is a great writer but not an artist. There are only about six artists among our prominent novelists. George Moore is one, though he writes, on the surface, damnably. But he can *see* like a poet. I greatly admire George Moore. If George Moore had been a South Sea trader and had learned grammar etc, he would have treated the sea as Conrad has treated it. I dare say this sounds odd, but it is profoundly true, and, for me, throws light on both men.

Some pages of *The Nigger* are exquisite in the extraordinary management of colour they display. But Conrad needs to curb his voracity for adjectives.

Have you ever read de Maupassant's *Etude sur Gustave Flaubert*, preface to *Bouvard et Pécuchet*—from which I quote above?[2] It is a most illuminating business, and one of the best bits of general literary criticism that I know of.

Sincerely yours

E. A. BENNETT

[1] In *Experiment in Autobiography*, in his assessment of Bennett as man and author, Wells wrote: "That unnecessary scrap of French is very Bennett. He was already deliberately heading for France and culture, learning French, learning to play the piano, filling up the gaps of a commonplace middle-class education with these accomplishments—and all with the brightest efficiency." (II, 626.)

[2] *Œuvres Complètes De Gustave Flaubert*, VII, 1885, pp. iii–lxvii. The phrase Bennett quotes is from the following paragraph:

6

WELLS TO BENNETT

Heatherlea

[*December* 1897]   *Worcester Park*

MY DEAR BENNETT

I'm glad you like Conrad. There's another swell budding. I've just been reading a proof of a book by Pugh [1] that's coming out sooner or later. *Tony Drum*'s the name of it and you look out for it!

Yours very faithfully

H. G. WELLS

"*Quand un homme, quelque doué qu'il soit, ne se préoccupe que de la chose racontée, quand il ne se rend pas compte que le véritable pouvoir littéraire n'est pas dans un fait, mais bien dans la manière de le préparer, de le présenter et de l'exprimer, il n'a pas le sens de l'art.*" (p. xlviii.)

[1] Edwin William Pugh (1874–1930). *Tony Drum*, 1898, is a story of the London slums.

7

BENNETT TO WELLS

24 *September* 1899   9 *Fulham Park Gardens, S.W.*[1]

MY DEAR WELLS,

A year or two ago we exchanged a few letters, and since then I have heard nothing from you, though I often hear *of* you from common friends—Roche, Lewis Hind, Eden Phillpotts etc.[2] I am writing now because I must—to congratulate you on the short stories in the *Pall Mall Magazine*,[3] which seem to improve as they go on, and which certainly strike me as being fine and in a very special sense *original* work. In this "prophetic" line of fiction, I will not say that I know nothing else so *strongly* imagined, but I will say that I know nothing else where the imagination is used with such virtuosity in the mani-

---

[1] Bennett rented a house for three years, 1897 to 1900, at this address.

[2] Walter Roche, a journalist; C. Lewis Hind (1862–1927), essayist and editor of the weekly, the *Academy*, former editor of the *Pall Mall Budget;* Eden Phillpotts (b. 1862), a contemporary novelist.

[3] From June to October the *Pall Mall Magazine* published in consecutive monthly issues "A Cure for Love," "The Vacant Country," "The Ways of the City," "Underneath," and "The Magnanimity of the Man of Pleasure," each one subtitled, "A Story of the Days to Come." They were reprinted in *Tales of Space and Time* (1899) as a single story entitled "A Story of the Days to Come," with the serial titles used as chapter-titles, the last being changed to "Bindon Intervenes."

pulation of material, or where the invention is so fresh, adroit and convincing. (And this despite the fact that I disagree (ferociously) with your general vision of the future of the race. Nor do I think that the changes you describe or any changes equally radical could occur in that fraction of time called a century.)

The September and October stories seem to me masterly. Do you not consider yourself fortunate, this time, in your illustrator? I gathered from a passage in *The War of the Worlds* [1] that you were not exactly enchanted with Warwick Goble's [2] efforts. Still, Goble is a very nice chap, with the most serious aspirations.

Among the 200 odd books that I have pretended to

[1] The passage is as follows: "I recall particularly the illustration of one of the first pamphlets to give a consecutive account of the war. The artist had evidently made a hasty study of one of the Fighting Machines, and there his knowledge ended. He presented them as tilted, stiff tripods, without either flexibility or subtlety, and with an altogether misleading monotony of effect. The pamphlet containing these renderings had a considerable vogue, and I mention them here simply to warn the reader against the impression they may have created. They were no more like the Martians I saw in action than a Dutch doll is like a human being. To my mind, the pamphlet would have been much better without them." (1898, p. 204.)

[2] Goble provided most of the illustrations for *The War of the Worlds* when it was published serially in *Pearson's Magazine*, April–December 1897. Fifteen of his illustrations were reproduced in the American edition of the book in 1898. Wells and his agent Pinker had tried to get illustrations in 1896 from Cosmo Rowe, a follower of William Morris and later a Fabian and rationalist. Only two of his illustrations, however, were used in *Pearson's* in the first instalment; one of these appeared as the frontispiece of the American edition.

review this year *The Sleeper*[1] has not found a place. But I shall be coming across it sooner or later, and shall expect it to be very excellent. If it is on the plane of the stories, I can't understand why it is only in its 8th thousand. (Or rather I *can* understand.)

I have heard of your illnesses in a vague way from time to time. I remember one lunch with J. N. Dunn[2] when he was awfully depressed about your bodily condition. I hope this business is now all over, and that you are able to work fair and square, unhandicapped.

Believe me
Sincerely yours
E. A. BENNETT

8

WELLS TO BENNETT

Arnold House[3]
Sandgate

25 *September* 1899   *Kent*

MY DEAR BENNETT,

I'm very glad indeed you like the *P.M.M.* stories and I only wish I could tell you *The Sleeper* was of the same

---

[1] *When the Sleeper Wakes*, 1899.

[2] James Nicol Dunn (1856–1919), editor of the *Morning Post*, 1897–1905.

[3] Wells was seriously ill in August 1898, spending a month convalescing in Kent. He was told, however, that he must live in a

quality. But it isn't. There's good stuff in it, but it's a big confused disintegrating thing. These *P.M.M.* stories derive enormously from Sullivan's [1] illustrations —not only the best *I* have had but the best I have seen to anyone's stories for a long time. Goble's a good chap no doubt but he made people think my tale was a wearisome repetition of kettles on camera stands. I really don't think he put a fair quantity of brain into that enterprise or I wouldn't have slanged him in the book.

It's tremendously kind of you to keep your eye on a man who has come into exile as I have. But don't you go grieving or permitting good men like Dunn to grieve over my bodily condition. The only consequence of my last year's convulsions is that I retain only one operative kidney and hence various small inconveniences and a restriction on the free violence of my exercises. I have to dine with caution and things like that. If none had a worse time than I—!

Yours very faithfully

H. G. WELLS

---

dry climate, on sand or gravel. Expecting to be an invalid, he had a house—Spade House—especially designed and built by C. A. F. Voysey. Before it was completed in December 1900, the Wellses occupied rented quarters in Sandgate.

[1] Edmund J. Sullivan (1869–1933).

9

WELLS TO BENNETT

Arnold House

15 *June* 1900   *Sandgate*

MY DEAR BENNETT,

I am glad indeed to hear you are ceasing that incongruous association with *Woman* and coming into the country to lead the austerer life and I was glad too that you had—with reservations—liked *Mr. Lewisham*[1] and that you prophesy a greater popularity for my poor books. But, if I may speak frankly and floridly, why have you,—in fact for emphasis—why the Hell have you joined the conspiracy to restrict me to one particular type of story? I want to write novels and before God I *will* write novels. They are the proper stuff for my everyday work, a methodical careful distillation of one's thoughts and sentiments and experiences and impressions. But that other stuff which you would have me doing day by day is no more to be done day by day than repartees or lyric poetry. The Imagination moves in a mysterious way its wonders to perform. I can assure you that I am *not* doing anything long and weird and strong in the vein of *The Time Machine* and I never intend to. I would as soon take hat and stick and start out into the

[1] *Love and Mr. Lewisham*, June 1900.

street to begin a passionate love. If it comes—well and good.

I shall look out for *Fame and Fiction*. I expect I shall find there certain articles I have read with very keen interest in the *Academy*.[1] I was at Rye the other day and *James* who has a fastidious palate for that sort of thing was commending one of them very highly, the one in which you pointed out the almost entire suppression of real sexual passion (as distinguished from the conventional process) in popular fiction, from the *Family Herald* upward.

Yours very faithfully
H. G. WELLS

10

WELLS TO BENNETT

5 *July* 1900   *Arnold House*
It's got to be the 14th   *Sandgate*
since I dated this.

MY DEAR BENNETT

I was very glad indeed to get your letter, and to find things are less at variance between us than I had supposed. But as for the Balzac theory no!—I don't hold with you

---

[1] These articles were later to appear in book form as *Fame and Fiction, an Inquiry into Certain Popularities*, 1901. The article referred to here is apparently "The Fiction of Popular Magazines," The *Academy*, 24 February 1900.

any more than I do with Garnett [1] and the Turgenev
theory or with the damned old art critics and the Michael-
Angelo–Raphael theory. In so far as any man's work
squares with the standards of any other man's work it
doesn't count. All fairly good work has its excellence
in something which is not commensurable with anything
outside itself. You not only cannot but you must not
attempt to make a criticism by instituting comparisons
or prescribing canons. No it is *not* "Balzac first and the
rest nowhere." Balzac is an Egyptian temple and damned
dark and stuffy in places to Turgenev's Corinthian
capitals, Dickens is a barn with astonishing gargoyles
and the English novel like the Gothic cathedral is too
big a thing for a complete specimen ever to get itself done.
For my own part I am a purblind laborious intelligence
exploring that cell of Being called Wells and I resent your
Balzac. But this sort of thing is more fitted for conversation than writing. I hope soon we may have some
chance of an argey bargey. Until when Believe me

Yours ever H. G. WELLS

I say—if it's not offensive—what was *your Mr. Lewisham*
called? [2] I can't find out and I want to read it.

---

[1] Edward Garnett (1868–1937), the critic, whose main occupation, as a reader for T. Fisher Unwin (and later for other publishers),
was the discovery and encouragement of unknown writers. David
Garnett, Edward's son, writes: "Indeed it was inconceivable to
Edward that he might be completely mistaken in a literary judgment." (*The Golden Echo*, London, 1953, p. 4.)

[2] Wells is referring to Bennett's *A Man from the North*, 1898.

II

WELLS TO BENNETT

Arnold House

30 *July* 1900   *Sandgate*

MY DEAR BENNETT,

My wife and I have read *A Man from the North* with the very keenest interest and we are both struck by the curious parallelism (in spite of their entire independence and authenticity) of the two books.[1] Your approach and line of thought are clearly rather more towards Gissing than are mine, and I am reminded by that, that Gissing some years ago when I was telling him the idea of *Lewisham* told me that he also had contemplated the same story. His title was to have been *The Common Lot*, and there you have as compactly as possible a certain difference in the point of view.

Do you ever do week-end raids out of London? If so, would you care to week-end here the third week-end in August (or later if that is engaged)? You can bathe from our garden-end and there are amusing and pleasant walks of from two miles to twenty—at our con-

---

[1] In both *A Man from the North* and *Love and Mr. Lewisham* the protagonist is drawn away from his dedicated career as, respectively, writer and scientist by romantic passion.

venience. There are also bands and promenades if that
is your game.

Yours very faithfully
H. G. WELLS

12

BENNETT TO WELLS

2 *August* 1900   9 *Fulham Park Gardens, S.W.*

MY DEAR WELLS,

I should like immensely to come down and have a day
or so with you. I oughtn't to, but I think I will. I think
I could come on Saturday 18th (if this is the week-end
you mean) strictly for the week-end. I am extended just
now over a Tillotson serial.[1] I have been 'laid aside' for a
month with an abscess, and am already late with delivery, but the benevolent syndicate has granted me an
extension of 6 weeks, bless it.

I write this letter from Burslem, whence I depart tonight, and where I have been observing the effect of the
Wesleyan Methodist Conference on the community. I
came down specially to observe the same, and have been
well rewarded. The public examination of candidates for
ordination, the other night at Longton, was one of the

---

[1] Lever Tillotson, a representative of the Bolton syndicate, which
bought serials and short stories for sale to provincial papers and
smaller weeklies. The serial referred to here is probably *The Grand
Babylon Hotel*, published in book form in 1902.

D

most genuinely *interesting* things that I have ever watched.[1]

It is enough for me that you and Mrs Wells were interested in *Man from the North*. There is much in it that is not authentic, merely fanciful, and quasi-sentimental—I can see now. But I seriously meant all of it at the time. It was the first work I did, and before I had finished it the technique thereof had advanced so much that I had to go back and write the first half again. So you may guess what it was to start with!

Well, I shall look forward to seeing you; and thanks very much for what in this district the élite call the 'invite'.   Sincerely yours

E. A. BENNETT

13

BENNETT TO WELLS

21 *August* 1900   9 *Fulham Park Gardens*

MY DEAR WELLS,

I am sure you will be relieved to hear that the bag and I caught that train. It was a great relief to me. The darned procession of vehicles was only 35 minutes late at Charing Cross—very good for the S.E.R. Excuse these facile sneers at the expense of your railway.

I have written 3,900 words today, played sundry piano

[1] This visit was to provide the detail for Bennett's treatment of Wesleyan Methodism throughout *Anna of the Five Towns*, 1902.

duets, and spent 3 hours at the office. By the way, I think that *Crimson Weed*[1] is 'not bad'. Such is my deliberate and elaborate view.

You and Mrs. Wells have done me a great deal of good —and incidentally disgusted me afresh with serials. I am in debt to you. Preoccupation with trains prevented me from being even decently civil to you when I parted from you yesterday, but perhaps you may be aware that I meant sundry unsaid things.

When I have got Dunstable[2] into order, will you and Mrs. Wells come and survey my acres and drive those horses that I am going to buy, and oscillate between those apple trees? Anyhow I shall ask you, and if you don't there will be one feud the more in the literary world. I didn't mention to you that my sister and housewife is a literary cuss—writes, you know, books—and knows how to soothe the literary temperament in hours of domesticity. This by way of an inducement. I will let you know about S. Bowkett[3] in due course.

With kindest regards to Mrs. Wells and the author of the biology book.[4]   Yours

P.S. This isn't my own pen.   E. A. B.

[1] A novel by Christopher St John, published in July 1900.

[2] After his resignation from *Woman*, 5 June 1900, Bennett settled near Dunstable, Bedfordshire, at Trinity Hall Farm, Hockliffe, with his father and mother and his sister, Tertia. The chief reason for the move was the beginning of his father's last illness.

[3] Sidney Bowkett, a childhood friend of Wells, at this time a playwright. He was the original of Chitterlow in *Kipps*.

[4] A reference to Wells's *Text-Book of Biology*, 1893.

14

WELLS TO BENNETT

Arnold House

1 *September* 1900   *Sandgate*

MY DEAR BENNETT.

What will you give us if we don't send you your photograph? [1] We haven't printed it yet but the negative looks good for a fiver to me.

Yours ever

H. G. WELLS

Anyhow they ain't "pretty."

15

WELLS TO BENNETT

Arnold House

19 *October* 1900   *Sandgate*

MY DEAR BENNETT.

I have nothing to say but as a literary man I see no reason in that why I should not write. The Missus and

---

[1] Wells was an enthusiastic photographer at this time. In a letter of 13 December 1899 J. B. Pinker, Wells's literary agent, wrote to him, "I hope you won't get influenza as it would interrupt your photography." The photograph of Bennett referred to in Wells's letter is very probably the one reproduced as the frontispiece of this volume.

me are doing well and we hope you are the same.   They are putting in our casements. *Lord Jim* is out and that reminds me that Christopher St. John is not Conrad's "Sinjohn" but another.[1]

> God bless and keep you
> is ever the Prayer
> of yours ever
> H. G. WELLS

16

WELLS TO BENNETT [*Postcard*]

> *Spade House*

[Postmark 8 *December* 1900]   *Sandgate*

Got there at last!   No carpets no dining room table or chairs, little food but still—*there*!

> Yours ever
> H. G.

---

[1] John Sinjohn was the pseudonym used by John Galsworthy in his first two novels, *Jocelyn*, 1898, and *Villa Rubein*, 1900, and two books of short stories, *From the Four Winds*, 1897, and *A Man of Devon*, 1901. Galsworthy and Conrad had met in 1893 when Galsworthy was a passenger on an English ship of which Conrad was first mate. Conrad was a sympathetic critic of Galsworthy's early work.

17

WELLS TO BENNETT

Spade House
1 *June* 1901　　　　　　　　　　　　　　　*Sandgate*

MY DEAR BENNETT.

It is a pity you will keep up this foolishness about Dickens, but time and reflection may temper you and lead to something nearer wisdom. Gissing who is here and I am afraid very gravely ill at last [1] tells me he has nothing to add to his *Charles Dickens* which if you haven't read you ought to read (pub. by Blackie). And my dear man, if you possibly can get your hands on it, read *By the Ionian Sea* just published by Chapman & Hall. I would be glad indeed if for once Gissing could have a shout. This book deserves it mightily and if it does not get it— Gissing may perhaps never hear a shout. "*Verbum sap*" I believe is the sort of thing one says at this point.

I shall be glad indeed to read that SERIOUS novel [2] and I shall look for that series of articles.[3] There is a coolness between myself and Hind [4] quite outside literary matters

[1] On 25 June 1901 Gissing wrote to Mrs Wells from a tuberculosis sanatorium.

[2] *Anna of the Five Towns*, 1902.

[3] "The Fallow Fields of Fiction," by Bennett, appeared in three parts in the *Academy*, 15 June, 29 June, 20 July 1901.

[4] See note 2, p. 41.

and I am sorry to find it affects criticism. I'll read *Resurrection* [1]—I want something to read. In this matter of Visiting—Visiting and receiving are alike 'off' for us just now for Mrs. Wells and I have been collaborating (and publication is expected early in July) in the invention of a human being.[2]

The Lord bless and keep you and lighten your black bad Dickensless mind.   Yours ever

              H. G.

18

BENNETT TO WELLS

Trinity Hall Farm
Hockliffe
3 *June* 1901   *Bedfordshire*

MY DEAR WELLS,

You and Mrs. Wells have my best wishes for the future. I am sorry to hear of Gissing's illness. I was in town last week, and could have arranged to review his two books then, but never thought of it. Hind gives me everything I ask for provided early birds like Lucas [3] haven't stepped in beforehand and skimmed the cream off the week's milk. Living out here, I am somewhat at a disadvantage

---

[1] By Tolstoy, published in England in 1900.

[2] The Wellses' first son, George Philip, was born in July 1901.

[3] E. V. Lucas (1868–1938), at this time a member of the staff of the *Academy*.

in that respect. But I am sending to Hind to tell him Gissing is on my mind. There is a rhapsodic essay on him (Gissing—not Hind) in my new book.[1] Truly I don't think that Hind's personal relations with you have affected criticism. When he choked me off you, he had recently done or caused to be done a screed on you "as prophet." [2] and I remember thinking at the time he was editorially right in declining an "enquiry" into you at that moment. To err is human and Hind takes full advantage of his humanity—even to allowing himself to be imposed upon by that literary fraud, Charles Marriott, author of *The Column*,[3]—but I have found him singularly and rather finely careless of anything except (what he considers) literary justice. Such is my testimony.

I perceive you couldn't keep your new house out of the *Fortnightly*! This third article is the best yet.[4] I have never seen so good an illustration of the scientific use of imagination.

Touching Gissing, do you think he will ever get a real "shout"? I think not. What matter? The consciousness

[1] *Fame and Fiction.*

[2] "A Novelist of the Unknown" (unsigned), the *Academy*, 23 June 1900.

[3] Published in 1901. *The Column* is a highly symbolic novel, laid in Cornwall, where the heroine's father has set up a Doric column, which becomes the symbol of his daughter's cult of nature and the elements.

[4] Part III of *Anticipations* in the 1 June 1901 issue of the *Fortnightly Review.*

of the man who has written *Demos* must be a fairly satis-factory possession. Show him the enclosed if you care to.[1] Or rip it up; it is a spare proof. I don't know whether vanity or a desire to give him a small satisfaction makes me send it.

My kindest regards to your wife,

Yours

E. A. B.

19

BENNETT TO WELLS

Trinity Hall Farm

Hockliffe

22 *July* 1901

MY DEAR WELLS,

Appropos of a par. in the *Chronicle*, my hearty con-gratulations to you and Mrs. Wells.[2] I hope things still go quite well.

Your sincerely

E. A. BENNETT

[1] The essay referred to earlier in the letter.
[2] On the birth of their first child.

20

WELLS TO BENNETT

Spade House

19 *August* 1901   *Sandgate*

PRIVATE AND ABUSIVE

MY DEAR BENNETT.

I really don't see why you should have your book [1] sent to me unless it is to draw my attention to the fact that so far as you are concerned I don't exist. After all we exist to be ourselves and it would be a mere affectation for me to pretend to take an impersonal interest in a book which professes to be a review of the state of contemporary fiction. With the people in an omnibus it would be convenient to pretend I didn't care a damn for my public reputation and acceptance but it would be silly not to admit to you that these things are primary things in my life. I take your book therefore at first at any rate as a landscape in which I ought to figure, and I *don't* figure! [2] It is written altogether without reference to me. And so far as that goes it seems to me rather unintelligent and commonplace. I am an absolutely unique figure in

---

[1] *Fame and Fiction,* 1901.

[2] Bennett deals largely with extremely popular novelists like Miss Braddon, J. M. Barrie, and Rhoda Broughton. He devotes the last three chapters, however, to Gissing, Turgenev, and George Moore respectively.

contemporary literature, I am relevant to the criticism of prose writing and prose reading in more directions than any other man who writes and to keep me out of the picture is simply to show that you have the sort of mind that cannot take in a new thing until someone else has put it to you. For example you are all wrong about the Fiction of the Popular Magazines on account of your failure to grasp ME. The *Strand Magazine* pays £125 for a short story by me and *Pearson's* £15 a thousand for *The Sea Lady* [1] and Ray Lankester [2] will tell you I've never jarred on the exacting sensibilities of a critical scientific mind. This has nothing to do with art, but it smashes your article and it shows a want of knowledge even of that low sort that deals with material facts. That particular issue however is a minor one. It is the last three chapters that get at ME most intimately, that make me— in view of the fact that you will probably go on writing and influencing opinion through all the years of my development—lift up my clenched hands and say, "Oh damn this Bennett!" There is a blindness to certain qualities that puts you, so far as they are concerned, outside the elect, a tone deafness. You so manifestly are not

[1] *The Sea Lady* was serialized in *Pearson's Magazine*, July–December 1901.

[2] Edwin Ray Lankester (1847–1929), at this time Director of Natural History Departments and Keeper of Zoology, British Museum. He was soon to be recognized as an authority on zoology, and was knighted in 1907. He was also to be a consultant to Wells in the writing of *The Outline of History*.

up to Turgenev any more than you are up to Dickens or *Love and Mr. Lewisham*. You have been told about Turgenev. You talk about his temperament and his artistry, but you know you don't see the beauty he sought and gained any more than you get that indefinable quality of the point of view, that humour, that makes Dickens, for all his crimes, so dear to us in places. (Consequently you will always miss me in my novels, as I do them). Does it not occur to you that when you and Garnett solemnly set aside Turgenev's own preference among his books, you may after all do no more than indicate your personal quality? And because you miss there subtle elements and aim to achieve criticism by pure intelligence, you overrate the gawky crowded exploits of Balzac and Gissing and of such merely ambitious persistent intelligent persons as George Moore. Well, well. For me you are part of the Great Public, I perceive. I am doomed to write 'scientific' romances and short stories for you creatures of the mob, and my novels must be my private dissipation. "Damn this Bennett!" I say, with all my heart, and am, my dear Bennett,

Yours ever

H. G. WELLS

21

BENNETT TO WELLS

Trinity Hall Farm
16 *October* 1901   *Hockliffe*

MY DEAR WELLS,

I sent you my "bright" and amusing book as a return —feeble, but the best I could do—for the copy of *Love and Mr. Lewisham* which you caused to be sent to me. I hesitated seven days and seven nights before sending it. I kept saying to myself: "Now will the incurable and amazing modesty of this great man prevent him from guessing the true reason why I have left him out of this my book?" (which however does not pretend to be a "review of the state of contemporary fiction.") I at last resolved to send it and hope for the best. Alas! The worst has happened. You will have to see a doctor about that modesty of yours. Can you not perceive that I left you out

a. Because I felt incompetent to assess you.
b. Because nothing less than a whole book could contain you.
c. Because your popularity needs no explaining, being the obvious reward of merit.
d. Because it was my ambition, after 25 years of study,

meditation and prayer, to attempt an elaborate monograph on you, and let this be the climax of my career.

You *did* perceive these reasons, revered friend. But again your modesty, by a curious intensification of itself, refused to let you admit them.

Your views about my views of Gissing, Moore, and Turgenev, leave me cold, having regard to your own article on Gissing in the *Fortnightly*,[1] and to the fact, universally recognized by press and public, that on Moore and Turgenev I am the first and only authority in this country. Nobody else knows anything about these two writers except me, and when I ope my lips I expect a hushed nation to listen and acclaim. Still, in the future, I shall probably surpass even myself on these writers.

'So on my heels a fresh perfection tread,' as Keats said, evidently with me in mind.

I note lately the evidence of an extraordinary activity on your part. Perhaps you have observed how difficult it is to pick up a decent magazine without You in it. I look in the *Fortnightly* and the *Strand* in order to run even with you. And now damned if you haven't let me in for *Pearson's*! And I hear rumour of a "Dream of Armageddon" in something else.[2] You make your

[1] Bennett is apparently referring to Wells's "The Novels of George Gissing," the *Contemporary Review*, August 1897. Search has failed to reveal an article by Wells on Gissing in the *Fortnightly Review*.

[2] *Black and White*.

readers work. What I hunger for is the successor to *L. and Mr. L.* I will make a meal off that, I promise you. I will rend it to pieces, (and remember that I am not precisely Lieut. Col. Eustace Balfour) [1] for sternness is the highest compliment one can pay to that work which its author regards most seriously. (Dr. Johnson.)

My kindest regards to your wife, and I trust you all flourish.

Yours in all art and culture

E. A. BENNETT

[1] In the December 1900 issue of the *Fortnightly Review* an article by Wells, "The Cyclist Soldier," attacked the *Cyclist Drill* of 1900, a government pamphlet concerning the military use of bicycles. Lt. Col. Eustace Balfour, the "not very athletic senior" of Wells's article and one of the authors of the *Cyclist Drill*, took violent exception to Wells's charges in "Military Cycling, after Mr. Wells" in the February 1901 issue of the *Fortnightly*. Wells, however, apparently had the last word in a letter, "The Soldier Cyclist," which appeared in the March issue of the magazine, although he complained in a letter of 6 February 1901 to J. B. Pinker that the editors should have printed his reply to Balfour as an article instead of relegating it to the correspondence section. "Damn the Empire of bloody idiots! As you know I don't want pay, I don't even want credit in the matter, I simply want to ventilate a dangerously stuffy corner."

22

WELLS TO BENNETT

Spade House

17 *October* 1901   *Sandgate*

MY DEAR BENNETT.

I hope you are serious when you speak of my greatness, because it is a very serious matter to me. Naturally you don't understand that aspect of the Question, except by hearsay. Owever——

I'm really *not* producing violently but several things have come out this year that have been hanging about. V'la toot! Mainly just now I'm meditating on a something which is really this time to get me all together and reconcile all my aspects—something in the form of a lax extravaganza of the Rabelais type (you understand I don't mean indecency by the name of J. F. R.) superposed on interlocutors such as one gets in *Tristram Shandy*—discourses and Peacockian dialogue—an effect of looking into a room in which a number of human beings behave and talk, with someone like Father Shandy giving a lantern entertainment with comments.[1] Do you see it at all?

Yours ever,

H. G.

---

[1] This letter very probably represents Wells's earliest notion of the form of *Boon*. The first dated section of manuscript of *Boon* was written on 1 July 1905, although the book was not published until 1915.

23

WELLS TO BENNETT

Spade House
[21 *November* 1901]   *Sandgate*
MY DEAR BENNETT.

My modesty *forces* me to send you *Die Zeit* with an
article by one Graz [1] that seems really to display some
inkling of my real greatness. I am much gratified thereby.

Yours ever

H. G.

24

BENNETT TO WELLS

Trinity Hall Farm
23 *November* 1901   *Hockliffe*
MY DEAR WELLS,

Neither of your books has come my way, reviewing.
For one thing Hind always keeps these plums for him-
self, and my ladies' paper is not interested in publicism.
I have read *The First Men in the Moon* in *Strand*,[2] and

[1] Fr. Graz, "H. G. Wells," *Die Zeit* (Wien), No. 364.
[2] *The First Men in the Moon*, the *Strand Magazine*, December
1900 to August 1901. Bennett indicates the title by a sketch of
three small men in a new moon.

E

hasten to insult and annoy you by stating that the last two instalments are among the very best things you have done. I have read *Anticipations* in *Fortnightly*, and hasten to say that I have been absolutely overwhelmed by the breadth and the sheer intellectual vigour of them, not to mention the imaginative power. These articles really have made me a little afraid of you. Either you have in a supreme degree the journalistic trick of seeming omniscience, or you are one of the most remarkable men alive. And I say this plainly, without any undercurrent of fun. The only fault that I have found with these articles is that *occasionally* there appeared to be a certain turgidity, or confusedness, which struck one as though it might have been avoided either by greater length of explanation, or by severe re-writing. It was as though you had tumbled some of the stuff out of a flowing bowl, like Dumas. I gather from a review that the conclusion of the book has not been printed in the *Fortnightly*—and this the most interesting part of the book. For this reason I should like the book. I had meant to buy it (sinning against my principle of never buying new books), but if I can get it for nothing I can put the price into the missionary box.

With my London-Matric knowledge of German I have struggled through the appreciation of you in *Die Zeit*. I see the writer lights on most of the things that I have singled out for you.

Have you read the first Realistic Scotch Novel—*The*

House with the Green Shutters? [1] It is not first-class, but
it is glorious after Barrie, Maclaren, Crockett and Co.[2]
You see Scotland in it for the first time in your life.

Yours,

E. A. B.

25

WELLS TO BENNETT

Spade House

25 *November* 1901   *Sandgate*

MY DEAR BENNETT.

I am glad to tell you your modest surmise is correct.
There is no illusion. I *am* great. And the detached reading of *Anticipations* gives you no inkling of the massive
culminating effect of the book as a whole. I am asking
C & H to send you a copy,[3] but the mean suspicion of
publishers that authors use their numerous presentation
copies as personal gifts may stand in the way. In which

---

[1] By George Douglas, pseudonym of G. D. Brown (1869–1902).
Published in 1901.

[2] Ian Maclaren, pseudonym of John Watson, 1850–1907 (*Beside
the Bonnie Brier Bush*, 1894), and Samuel Rutherford Crockett,
1860–1914 (*The Stickit Minister*, 1893), both, along with Barrie,
sentimental novelists of humble Scottish life. Wells had expressed
his bitter contempt for the Kailyard School when he was reviewing
fiction for the *Saturday Review*, 1895–1897.

[3] *Anticipations* ran serially in the *Fortnightly Review*, April–
December 1901. It was published in book form by Chapman &
Hall in November 1901.

case I will honestly get the book and send it you myself. I want you to read it very much *and*, if it takes you, to do something to propagate my gospel. I believe quite simply that a real first class boom and uproar and discussion about this book will do an infinite amount of good in the country and to you at least there is no need to put my belief in breeches. I think I am safe to get most of the comfortable *educated* London public, but I dream of getting it read by parsons and country doctors and all that sort and going much wider than my publishers dream. I think there are a multitude of interesting quotes to be dug out of the book, about home conveniencies, the status of unmarried girls, cooking in the future, building, dress etc, that ought to [be] *ground-bait* for the big public even—the Corellian public. (Some of the more denunciatory passages by the bye, when I read them over again strike me as singularly like Marie.) I think you are right about that turgidity in places—but the thing has been a hell of a handful to manage.

Yours ever

H. G.

26

WELLS TO BENNETT

26 *November* 1901   *Spade House*
                                        Sandgate
MY DEAR BENNETT

Could you do a week end (or mid week if it suits you
better) here *soon*. I've been hoping to persuade you to
come down for some time and something has arisen that
might enable you to be of very great service to the Conrads—without any inconvenience to yourself. What of
Saturday week? Saturday to Monday next the room's
took but any other time——.   Yours ever

                                        H. G.

27

WELLS TO BENNETT

[*December* 1901]   *Spade House*
                                        Sandgate
MY DEAR BENNETT.

Have you read "Amy Foster" in *Illustrated London
News*? [1] If not I'll lend you Conrad's copies. *Very*
interesting.   Yours ever

                                        H. G.

---

[1] "Amy Foster," a short story by Joseph Conrad, appeared
serially in the 14, 21, and 28 December 1901 issues of the *Illustrated
London News*.

28

BENNETT TO WELLS

Trinity Hall Farm
13 *December* 1901 *Hockliffe*

MY DEAR WELLS,

That fat bus driver prefers the interior of your house to the exterior, and the inhabitants thereof to either. He kept on saying, when the talk flagged, that no one would expect such a nice inside—to look at the outside. I explained to him that that particular sort of house was quite the fashion just now, and might be observed in large numbers up and down Surrey. But that didn't seem to make him like it any better. His final conclusion was, damn the house, but if folks in general was a bit more like you and Mrs, folks in general would be a lot better "served."

Following your advice yesterday I did no work because I didn't feel inclined to. This is bad for me, and I must request you not to offer such advice in future.

That detective play ought to be called simply *The Crime*.[1] Chapman Hall haven't sent *Uncle's-dissipations*[2] yet. I can see I shall have to buy that book in order to do

---

[1] A projected play to be written in collaboration by Bennett and Wells, eventually entitled *The Crime*. It was never completed.

[2] *Anticipations*. "Uncle" was a humorous appellation Bennett and Wells occasionally applied to each other.

it any good, and after all, that is rather a neat way of
doing a book good. I had a letter from Phillpotts yesterday, in which he enthuses over the book (and his restricted literary sympathies do not urge him to read much
of your work); it is the final chapters which impress him.
He is very great on Malthus and the annihilation of the
unfit and all that sort of thing. But the point is that your
book has caught hold of him; "gripped him by the belly",
as Stead [1] told Carlyle God had gripped the liver of
Darlington.

Don't forget to tell Pinker about the undersigned.[2]

Your company has jerked my brain into a state of un-
holy activity. With best respects to Mrs. H. G.

Yours ever
E. A. B.

[1] William Thomas Stead (1849–1912), editor of the *Review of
Reviews*. Stead was a journalist crusader with such books as
Maiden Tribute of Modern Babylon, 1885, and *If Christ Came to
Chicago*, 1893. At one time Stead was editor of the *Northern Echo*,
which was published at Darlington in Durham

[2] In a letter dated 12 December 1901 Pinker thanks Wells for
"sending Bennett along. I think I can do something for him."
Pinker was to serve as Bennett's literary agent until his (Pinker's)
death in 1922.

29

WELLS TO BENNETT

8 *February* 1902

MY DEAR E.A.B.

I want very much to come and gossip at Hockliffe but not with an article of this sort in the air.[1] I find this attention to myself is getting at my peace of mind, making my egotism large and tender and generally doing me no good. I want to shut off that sort of thing. I've had a good pushful two months. Suppose you do the article and get it off first and then let me come and talk of decent things. What Walker [2] wants is pretty plain and simple.

---

[1] Bennett had contracted to do an article on Wells for the *Cosmopolitan Magazine*, meant, according to a letter from Pinker to Wells, 12 February 1902, "to prepare the way." The entire article is reprinted in Appendix B, p. 260. It was the first competent and conscientious critical appraisal of Wells's work. Wells had for some years been concerned with the failure of the American public to discern the serious and meaningful element in his writing. When *Anticipations* was being offered, he wrote to Pinker in January 1901, "Instead of trying to impress these blasted Americans with the idea that I'm something smart and snappy, why don't you insist upon my literary position, my translations in particular and my standing abroad? . . . Don't you understand the whole thing will *mean* something?"

[2] John Brisben Walker, a representative of the *Cosmopolitan Magazine*. On 6 November 1901 Wells signed a memorandum of agreement with Walker granting *Cosmopolitan* the American rights on "any work in the nature of a story or novel and having a length

Instead of wanting me to advertise myself like bloody-
asses like Chapman & Hall do, he wants to advertise me.
I suppose he's going to run this article wide and extensive
to clear the road for the stuff which is to follow in the line
of *Anticipations*. At present no decent article on me, no
decent criticism (not a column of reviewing even) has
ever appeared about me in America. The great American
public has for the most part never heard of me. Para-
graphs circulate to the effect that I was a "dry goods
clerk" and I class with George Griffith[1] as a purveyor of
wild "*pseudo*" scientific extravaganza. The reviewer of
books in America—he appears to get printed in among
the dentifrice advertisements—like the very lowest class
reviewer in this country says with an airy confidence that
I "outrage every probability of science" and things like
that. "English Jules Verne" is my utmost glory. You
are not dealing with an intelligent public which finds me
interesting and wants me solidly placed, you are dealing
with gross, stupid ignorance and what you say—since

you will say it well—will pitch the key of criticism for
the next year at any rate. I'd be grateful if you'd remember that. Stupid praise at this juncture would do me vast

greater than ten thousand words which the said H. G. Wells may
complete and have ready for serial publication after the date of this
agreement until the end of the year 1902."

[1] George Chetwynd Griffith (d. 1906), a sensational novelist,
who wrote such novels as *A Honeymoon in Space*, 1901, and *The
World Masters*, 1903.

harm, insincere advertisement exaggeration of what I am. But I do honestly regard myself as a First Class Man, one of the first hundred writing in English now—I believe you do—and there's a certain full dress and high class way of writing of a man which Walker wants and I think the situation wants. You'll do the particular thing much better if you don't discuss it with me. There's a dozen things I can imagine usefully said and that I think you'd be willing to say, but whether you get them into this article or not depends entirely on the line you take in writing. They'd be better left out than stuck in. There's a quality in the worst of my so-called "pseudo-scientific" —(imbecile adjective) stuff that the American doesn't master which differentiates it from Jules Verne, e.g. just as Swift is differentiated from fantasia—isn't there? There is something other than either story writing or artistic merit which has emerged through the series of my books, something one might regard as a new system of ideas—"thought". It's in *Anticipations* especially Ch IX and it's in my Royal Institution Lecture[1] and it's also in *The First Men in the Moon* and *The Invisible Man* and Chaffery's chapter in *Love and Mr. L.*[2] That's as much as I can say to you in this matter if we talked all day. If so

[1] "The Discovery of the Future," delivered 24 January 1902, and published in February 1902.

[2] *Love and Mr. Lewisham*, chapter 23. In these references one can find the early development of Wells's idea of a natural aristocracy of talent and intellect, which he later expressed in the Samurai, the New Republic, and the Open Conspiracy.

be there is a chance of a casual allusion to Huxley who was my professor at the Royal Coll. of Science or to the R. Institution or to my first class honours B.Sc. Lond. or to my translated editions in French, German, Italian, Spanish, Norwegian, Hungarian, Czech and Danish, there's no need to be secretive. You are dealing with a damned ignorant snobbish public and the "dry goods clerk" legend may just as well be mitigated as not. But if anything of that sort does come in, keep it in a corner.

To you Bennett I display the final confidence of shamelessness. It is nicer to write and dispatch this sort of thing than talk about it. You go and write your article and pack it off and we'll talk about that play and God and various things. I have an idea for a new sort of domestic drama—you see!

Also you are damned mean about presentation copies of *The Grand Babylon Hotel*[1]

Yours ever

H. G.

[1] Published January 1902.

30

WELLS TO BENNETT

Spade House

14 *February* 1902   *Sandgate*

MY DEAR BENNETT.

I think I've got something that will make

the Dramatic Sensation

of 1903.[1] I want to tell you about it. Can you come
down for a night sometime before next Thursday?

Yours ever

H. G.

P.T.O.

[*In Mrs Wells's handwriting*] And can you let us know
Mr. Whitton's (Whitten?)[2] spelling of his name and
initials?

A. C. W.

---

[1] *The Crime.*
[2] Wilfred Whitten, editor of *T.P.'s Weekly*, for which Bennett
was later to do an extended series of articles. Whitten was a col-
league of Bennett on the *Academy*.

3 I

WELLS TO BENNETT

Spade House
Sandgate

22 *February* 1902

MY DEAR BENNETT,

I don't altogether jump at *The Crime.* It's dissipation. Still if you do quite clearly mean to do all the work and let me come in "without hindrance to present occupation" it's tempting—wife and child—boots very old now —trousers so thin in seat as to give rise to chills—aged mother in the workhouse—mortgage on my bicycle— garden roller in pawn.

Yes

You get a commission for it and I'll give you seven clear days of honest collaboration.

Yours ever

H. G.

32

BENNETT TO WELLS

Trinity Hall Farm
24 *February* 1902   *Hockcliffe*

MY DEAR WELLS,

Crime

I have communicated with both Harrison and Frohman's [1] man, and can get a double commission for this
play (England and America) upon producing a scenario
which contains nothing that the managerial mind considers too startling. In a few days I shall produce that
scenario, and as I shall be in London next week (toward
the end) I think I should run down and submit it to you
first. I shan't want you to put me up. You might, if convenient, give me half a day out of the allotted seven.
$7 - \frac{1}{2} = 6\frac{1}{2}$. I could write the piece by myself in 7 days.

Harrison has invited me to adapt an old English
comedy for the Haymarket and terms are now arranged.

Yours

E. A. B.

[1] Frederick Harrison (d. 1926), co-manager, with Cyril Maude,
of the Haymarket Theatre, 1896–1905. Charles Frohman was an
American theatrical producer.

33

BENNETT TO WELLS

Trinity Hall Farm

26 *March* 1902   *Hockliffe*

MY DEAR H. G.

Despite its opening phrase, the *Débâts* article might have been much worse than it is. There is some pretty wit in it. I had always looked on Filon [1] as rather a bore.

Somewhat depressed today by the thought of Pinker in peril on the boundless deep for our profit and advancement. He wasn't over-struck by my article on you,[2] which I reckon as rather a good sign of its real excellence.

I trust you are better.

Yours,

A. B.

[1] Pierre Marie Augustin Filon, French literary critic.
[2] For the *Cosmopolitan Magazine*.

34

BENNETT TO WELLS

6 *June* 1902   *Trinity Hall Farm*
                                  Hockliffe

MY DEAR WELLS,

A young friend of mine of the name of Humberstone,[1] a person of some parts, including obstinacy and enterprise, has conceived a *Schoolmasters Year-Book* and has got Swan Sonnenschein to run it. The annual is to contain some special articles, and Humberstone wants an article from you. In discussing the book with me he asked me if I would "pave the way" for him with you. I said I would write to you, and lo! I have written to you. I informed him that your stuff had to be paid for a tidy bit. He wants you to write about anything that is dear to you.

If you are disposed to consider this matter, I will tell the youth to do his own business with you direct.

Here endeth this paving letter.

                               Yours

                               E. A .B.

P.S. I have just read *The Sleeper* for the first time. You make a great mistake in condemning it. But literary criticism was never your forte.

                  Kindest regards to Mrs. H.G.

                               A. B.

---

[1] Thomas Lloyd Humberstone. Swan Sonnenschein and Co. Ltd was a publishing company. *The Schoolmaster's Yearbook and Directory* appeared annually until 1915.

35

WELLS TO BENNETT

Spade House

8 *June* 1902   *Sandgate*

MY DEAR BENNETT.

We're just off to Switzerland and I've exhausted my poor little brains on the first half of the stuff that is to follow up *Anticipations* in the *F.R.*[1] I'm afraid I'd not be able to do anything for this cove. He'd find the editors of the *School World* very friendly and useful I think. Ask him to send me a form by the bye. I'm an ex secondary schoolmaster with degrees and things.

Yours ever

H. G.

He ought to ask Professor Perry [2] for an article on mathematical teaching and A. T. Simmons [3] of the *School World* for one on science work.

[1] *Mankind in the Making* appeared in the *Fortnightly Review*, from September 1902 to September 1903.

[2] John Perry (1850–1920), Professor of Mechanics and Mathematics, Royal College of Science.

[3] Arthur Thomas Simmons (1865–1921), joint editor of the *School World*. Simmons was an old friend of Wells's days at the Normal School of Science in South Kensington.

36

WELLS TO BENNETT

Spade House

3 *July* 1902   *Sandgate*

MY DEAR BENNETT.

Get hold if you can of H. B. Marriott Watson's *Godfrey Merivale*.[1] It's quite a new departure for him—in the *Man from the North* vein. I think you may like it extremely. The last 30 pages cook up amazing. You see.

Yours ever

H. G.

---

[1] Henry Brereton Marriott Watson (1863–1921). *Godfrey Merivale, a Portion of His History* was published in May 1902. Watson was a prolific writer of romances. He was an assistant editor of *Black and White* and the *Pall Mall Gazette*, and had also served on the *National Observer* under W. E. Henley. It was Watson who introduced Wells to Henley.

37

WELLS TO BENNETT

Spade House
Sandgate

2 September 1902

MY DEAR BENNETT.

I've just read the *Cosmopolitan* article[1] and I am enormously satisfied. This sort of thing like a theatrical poster has to enhance, but allowing for that, it takes me as being really good. It keeps what I imagine to be a likeness in spite of the enlargement; it is acutely sympathetic. Accept I pray you my warmest thanks. And also for putting me on to that quite brilliantly done and (as Dr. Rob^n Nicoll[2] would say) most unpleasant book, *Le Journal d'une Femme de Chambre*.[3] We don't turn out a book a year over here on the level of that work as work. One came out of it like Falstaff out of the buck basket.

Yours ever

H. G.

[1] E. A. Bennett, "Herbert George Wells and His Work," August 1902. See Appendix B, p. 260.

[2] Sir William Robertson Nicoll (1851–1923), a Scottish man of letters and Free Church Minister, founder of the *Bookman*.

[3] By Octave Mirbeau (1848–1917), published in 1900. Mirbeau was a radical journalist and dramatist, at one time a member of Zola's group.

38

WELLS TO BENNETT

Spade House

9 *September* 1902   *Sandgate*

MY DEAR BENNETT

Anna[1] to hand. I will do my duty by her and you. Meanwhile learn that *The Wings of the Dove* is a book to read in and learn from. There are things in it *you* couldn't do, *I* couldn't do, nobody could do but James. Some are defects—some aren't. Anyhow I would give an oceanful of *Octopuses*[2] and a bloody suburb full of *Houses with Green Shutters* and all George Moore whatsoever for this book, which I will honestly confess I have not at present read through.

Yours ever

H. G.

If I wasn't so pressed I'd do a few remarks in the Educational press.

————————

The Sleeper has a broken back and a swollen rump.—*You* don't know.

————————

Address. Poste Restante *Faido* next week. Then *Locarno.*

[1] *Anna of the Five Towns*, 1902.
[2] *The Octopus: a Story of California*, 1901, by Frank Norris, a novel of the exploitation of California farmers and their products by a railway system.

39

WELLS TO BENNETT

Spade House

9 *September* 1902　　　　　　　　　　　　*Sandgate*

MY DEAR BENNETT,

Anna is very good indeed—a good picture of the Pottery culture (or want of it) full of incidental interest and interesting as a story. The characters strike me as real, consistent and individual, Mynors perhaps a little *hard* and flat, not quite modelled, a little touch of personal vanity—about the shape of his nose for example—would have rounded him off—but the rest all there. Your style is not of course my style and there's not three consecutive sentences I should let stand if I had the rewriting of it, but that is partly individual difference. Partly it isn't. Partly it is that—blessed thought!—you are not yet artistically adult, Gissing and George Moore and the impersonal school and a certain consciousness of good intentions are evident—it is not suggestive of the ease and gusto and mastery of your Potters with the clay for example, it isn't nearly so easy and engaging and *good* as the stuff you have been writing in the *Academy* [1]—so far as style goes. For example, down here you told a story about "hanging

[1] *The Truth About an Author* ran in the *Academy* anonymously from 3 May to 2 August 1902.

about a chapel on the offchance of a service" and you told it in just the note. It was enjoyed and remembered. In your story that comes in inopportunely with no sense of enjoyment. On the whole I should describe my impression as being that of a photograph a little underdeveloped. It is most underdeveloped towards the end. There you have arranged a series of very finely planned and I (as an experienced workman) know, finely imagined, emotional scenes. And they don't *tell* for a quarter what they are worth. The visit of Anna and Mynors to the Price home is cardinal. It ought to be charged with emotion. It ought to be immense. It was worth writing over and over again, it was worth sweating blood to do well. Good lines of course in abundance—the last on 341 for example [1]—but as a whole? You reach the top of the book (and it's fairly high) in the Isle of Man. From the death of Titus Price onward you are not all you will someday be (D.V.)   But the way you tip W. P.[2]

[1] "The next day Sarah Vodrey [the Price's servant] died—she who had never lived save in the fetters of slavery and fanaticism. After fifty years of ceaseless labour, she had gained the affection of one person, and enough money to pay for her own funeral. Willie Price took a cheap lodging with the woman who had been called in on the night of Sarah's collapse. Before Christmas he was to sail for Melbourne. The Priory, deserted, gave up its rickety furniture to a van from Hanbridge, where, in an auction-room, the frail sticks lost their identity in a medley of other sticks, and ceased to be. Then the bricklayer, the plasterer, the painter, and the paperhanger, came to the Priory, and whistled and sang in it." (London 1902.)

[2] Willie Price, Anna's young poverty-stricken lover, who at the end of the novel, is killed by a fall into a coal shaft.

down the coal shaft couldn't possibly be neater or better.

These are impressions. Don't take 'em to heart if they don't please you.

Yours ever

H. G.

I like the book out of comparison with *The G.B.H.*[1]—a mere lark that, as I said at the time.

40

WELLS TO BENNETT

Spade House

[18 *September* 1902]   *Sandgate*

MY DEAR BENNETT

I was struck with a perfectly vivid presentation of a play in *The Sea Lady* and I sent the book to Maude [2] (dead loss of 4/6 including postage) and suggested as much. The reply was as you will infer and he asked to see me on "another matter". Asked him, *what* other matter? V'la. Now what I say is this. No money, no more work, but if Maude will agree to stump up £200 (i.e. £100 each) on the play on delivery of the M.S. (stamped agreement) I'll put in a fortnight after Dec 1st 1902 this next December 1st i.e. I enclose my reply to him, which please seal and post.

[1] *The Grand Babylon Hotel*, 1902.
[2] Cyril Maude, actor and manager.

Anna I find ripens in the mind. I may have second thoughts about *Anna*.

Yours ever

H. G.

What reviews are you getting?

41

BENNETT TO WELLS

Trinity Hall Farm

20 *September* 1902   Hockliffe

MY DEAR H. G.

Knowing officially from you that for you 'no such thing as excellence exists,' I will not conceal my satisfaction at your remarks about *Anna*. I reckon no one in this isle knows more about the *craft* of fiction than you, except possibly me, and I am always struck by the shrewdness of your criticisms of novels from that point of view. But I think your notions about verbal style are fundamentally wrong, and nevertheless it just happens in this instance that what you say about my style is, I think, mainly correct. There *is* a 'certain consciousness of good intentions' that has jolly well got to disappear. Also I am inclined to agree that I am not yet artistically adult (at 35!)

I don't think the book falls off *much* after the death of old Price, and I think the emotional quality of the end is

as good as any. As to the under-developed photograph,
this is largely a matter of taste. But I trust you understand that the degree of development to which I have
brought the photograph, is what I think the proper degree. It is Turgenev's degree, and Flaubert's. It is *not*
Balzac's. Anyhow it is the degree that comes natural to
me. I note the possibility of your having second thoughts
about the book.

I have had no reviews worth mentioning yet.

Théâtre

What a pity you sent *The Sea Lady* to Maude! He is
utterly without judgment.

All right. I will make the state of the case plain to
Harrison myself. I scarcely fancy their enthusiasm will
carry them up to £200. But if it does, I am 'on'.

If it doesn't, I am prepared to offer to pay you half of
all I make out of *The Crime* up to £1,000, if you care to
turn it over to me absolutely. I have, personally, no
scruples about taking another man's ideas under the wing
of my own name in a case of this kind. But you may
object to such an arrangement. The suggestion is merely
a suggestion, and you have my leave to ignore it.

Remembrances to Mrs.

Yours

E. A. B.

42

WELLS TO BENNETT

Spade House

22 *September* 1902   *Sandgate*

MY DEAR BENNETT,

You'll come to a proper view of style by degrees and your attitude towards my criticisms shows nothing but the restiveness proper to a young man of spirit. I shall when the mood takes me reread the end of *Anna*.

I feel strongly that *The Crime* is rather too good a thing to drop. I think you make a fair offer about taking it over, but on the whole I'd rather I think see it through. But I don't see any chance of getting really to work at it until 1903. It's all nonsense to say it would only take me a week. I don't work that way. Suppose you go through it, amplify the scenario, get in some key lines and in fact write a sort of latticework of the play. Get this done in duplicate, send me a copy and use the other to negotiate. I'll turn the whole thing over in my mind and (if I may) come down to Hockliffe either in Dec 1902 or Jan 1903. I think we want a different relationship of the murderer and the woman. I feel if we let the thing go down to the subconscious for a bit it will come up stronger and richer.

Yours ever

H. G.

43

WELLS TO BENNETT

Spade House

27 *September* 1902   *Sandgate*

MY DEAR BENNETT

If you like we'll fix up for four days (to be dated exactly later) in the first week in December.

Not too much of *How to become an Author*—not too much of all that sort of thing. Cut your channel deeper.

Yours ever

H. G.

44

WELLS TO BENNETT

Spade House

14 *October* 1902   *Sandgate*

HON'D BENNETT.

The week begins Thursday Dec 4th when I arrive, and ends Monday Dec 8th when I depart.

God in his Mercy bless and keep you.

H. G. WELLS

45

WELLS TO BENNETT

[9 *December* 1902]   6 *Clements Inn* [1]

MY DEAR BENNETT

I arrived here about 12—in the middle of a large ball of dust, dirt, fluff and things indescribable. . . .[2] and I am going to buy a 12 h.p. Napier at the very earliest opportunity. I have burned to tell you of one very sad contray tom which has arisen to shadow the very pleasant stay I had with you. Jane it seems in early youth was alarmed or angered or something by 'a little white terrier dorg'. You see at once my melancholy predicament!

Your coat is being dealt with in a 40 h.p. carpet beating machine and hopes are entertained that it will be fit for packing tomorrow. Also your shirt. My Rumbrella has disappeared in these peregrinations. Either the motor-man (or Harrison, which considering what he wore is likelier) put my Rumbrella up his leg or you got my Rumbrella. If you got my Rumbrella *send* my Rumbrella. I shall be here until Saturday morning.

Yours ever

H. G.

[1] Wells kept a *pied-à-terre* here for about a year.
[2] Wells's dots.

46

WELLS TO BENNETT

Spade House

20 *August* 1903 *Sandgate*

MY DEAR BENNETT.

The Truth about an Author is literature; *Leonora* [1] as you will someday come to see is no more than a creditable performance. In the former you are saturated in knowledge, and the result is altogether happy. The latter—the latter is matter for discussion. The dreadful thing is the death of the husband, I don't see how you can forgive yourself that, and the subsequent petering out of the book. But anyhow you haven't wrung the guts of life though ever and again you get astonishingly near the illusion. One is impressed by the idea that the clever Bennett is going to be a fearful job for the artist Bennett to elude. "The Dance" for example is astonishingly neat and near, but it's fake. You've never been there. You impress me as knowing everything about Leonora except how it feels inside, and you've seen fit to write the book from inside. One is continually sitting back and saying Now *did* she do that? and deciding that it is not improbable she did. But one doesn't do that with a character that is really and truly *got*. With some of the people of

[1] 1903.

Thackeray and Dickens you say: "How like Becky (or whoever it is) to do that?" We aspire to exalted levels my friend and in that spirit I write. You do all sorts of subsidiary things in the book extraordinarily well. The nice shallow daughters (not the examinee who's not understood) (P.S. Jane says she is) the horrible vulgar social atmosphere (though done without the complete detachment one might like) David, the old uncle and his inside window, the father (excellent in his secrecy) many things like that couldn't be better. But Twemlow! Look here! I think the trouble is this. You're afraid of your principal characters. Twemlow hasn't modelling, he hasn't the unexpected inevitable thing about him that makes an individuality. He's all right everywhere—that is to say he is all wrong. He might have been made by combining all the virtues that get full votes in a committee on the upstanding manly commercial man of the world, and excluding everything else. You never met him Bennett. You'll say you've met him by the dozen perhaps. Which is exactly what I'm after.

Excuse my handwriting. I'm in bed with my beastly kidney again, and believe me.

Yours ever

H. G.

47

BENNETT TO WELLS

7 *Halsey House*
24 *August* 1903   *Red Lion Square*

MY DEAR H. G.,

Your letter robbed me of my afternoon's sleep today (I only got it this morning). I think your criticisms are usually tonic and wholesome for me. And you impress me fearfully sometimes—it may be your matter or your manner—I don't know which. I really do think you have a power of finding fault with fiction which I have not seen equalled. And yet I also feel that you are incapable of learning what I *know*, critically, of fiction. Your outlook is too narrow, and you haven't read enough. You still cling to the Dickens–Thackeray standards, and judge by them. As when you say: "How like Becky Sharp!" Would you say "How like Eugénie Grandet, or Madame Bovary, or Maisie?" The strongly marked character, the eccentric, the sharply-defined type, is the easiest thing in the world to do (you wouldn't believe how I despise my Meshach Myatt [1] as a creation) in such a manner that the reader can recognize all *his* acts for his. But the less typical can not, and ought not, to be done in this way, for

---

[1] The wealthy and eccentric uncle of Leonora's husband, John Stanway.

the reason that they are not so in life. It is in remarks like that that I think you give yourself away and impair the 'sanction' of what else you say. Far more important, have you grasped the fact that what I aim at is the expression of general moods, whether of a person or a whole scene, a constant 'synthetising' of emotion, before the elucidation of minor points of character? We should never be able to agree about the death of the husband. I take it you object to it because it is a sort of coincidence and because it solves (anyhow apparently) the difficulty of Leonora. I must talk to you sometime about coincidences in fiction and in life. The fact that this death solves a difficulty is to me entirely beside the point. It is a part of the inmost scheme of my book. I seem to think that the novelists who would object to it that it was too timely, are too proud to take the genuine material of life as they find it. Or they are afraid to. Because life is simply crammed full of such timelinesses. Personally, I think the stuff after the husband's death the best part of the book.

Quite beyond argument, you are wrong about Rose. She is dead right all through. I know the type as well as you do. Whatever the "dance" is, it is not fake. I have emphatically *been* there, and the thing is quite genuine, failure or not.

I fancy I shall make you a present of Twemlow, as I don't know whether I believe in him or not myself. When I began the book I didn't, but as I proceeded I gradually believed in him. The plot demanded an Anglo-American, and I simply invented him to meet the case exactly. I confess I have never met him. My brother (who is [a] good judge) said he was not convincing, but my sister (who is a better judge) is quite satisfied with him.

I feel in spite of my judgment that most of what you say is half true, in the annoying manner of half-truths. And I am much obliged to you for your candour (no one else will be so candid). I am conscious now of an intention to make you get down unconditionally on to your knees yet, in a future book. Of course I see you are dealing with the thing at an extremely high level, and that is all right. I do honestly wish, quite apart from this book, that I could fill you with a sense of your artistic limitations. No one, except Turgenev, ever had more technical skill than you have. But your perception of beauty is deficient; at least it isn't sufficiently practised and developed. However, go on and prosper

"My confidence is unabated," says Sir T. Lipton to-day.[1] So is mine. (This is rather fine humour, eh?)

[1] In the first race for the America's Cup on 23 August 1903 the *Reliable*, the American yacht, defeated the *Shamrock*, the British entry, owned by Sir Thomas Lipton. "Sir Thomas Lipton, on being interviewed by a representative of Reuter's Agency with regard to the race, said:—'We were beaten fair and square. It was splendid weather, and *Shamrock* did not do so well as I had expected she would in a race to leeward and return. My confidence in *Shamrock* is unshaken, and I hope she will yet make much better showing.'" (*The Times*, 24 August 1903.)

G

The Truth about an Author may be literature. But it isn't imaginative literature, and so cannot enter into the composition.

I hope this kidney trouble is nothing but what can be got over easily, and due merely to an imprudence. Let me know.

Yours ever

E. A. B.

48

WELLS TO BENNETT

Spade House

19 *September* 1903 *Sandgate*

MY DEAR BENNETT.

It's quite the best book [1] in its way and it's a orrible way. It will, thank God! be not of the slightest use to any human being. And no end will buy and read it. I believe, somewhere about the seat of your b——s, you conceal a caudal appendage of this description ∿. There is what would otherwise be an inexplicable infernality about you. Did you or did you not see, or did you sometimes get a sort of refracted sight and sometimes forget, the

[1] *How to Become an Author*, 1903.

humour of beginning with the Art of Spelling?[1] Passages read like a parody of Dr. Caliban.[2]

There is a more extraordinary first rate novel in all this.

Yours ever

H. G.

49

BENNETT TO WELLS

4 *rue de Calais* [3]

8 *October* 1903   *Paris*

MY DEAR H. G.,

Many thanks for *Mankind in the Making*.[4] Like *Anticipations* it is very wonderful, and very uneven. Some of the things in it are so excellent and so persuasive that they make one promise one's self to forgive you all your sins, past, present, and to come. All the criticism of the modern small home (p. 170 and thereabouts) is simply splendid. And I am very much struck indeed by your suggested 3 'courses' of Higher Education (p. 329 et seq.) and your

---

[1] Bennett's first chapter is actually entitled "The Literary Career." In Chapter II, "The Formation of Style," Bennett recommends in the first subdivision, "The Self-Education of the Aspirant," that the novice learn how to spell as a preliminary step.

[2] A reference to Hilaire Belloc's humorous book, *Caliban's Guide to Letters*, 1903.

[3] Bennett's home in Paris for more than three years of his protracted residence in France. He wrote here the novels *Leonora*, *A Great Man*, *Sacred and Profane Love*, and *Whom God Hath Joined*.

[4] September 1903.

general shelving of merely informational knowledge. Also by your schemes for, and defence of, authors. Also by the close of the book. Much of the book is really *human*. At the same time I will not conceal from you that I often thought of your reference to 'jerry-building' on p. vi as being decidedly to the point, and that to confess a sin is not to excuse it. As with *Anticipations* I think the book might have been much better if you had put more 'back' into it. You replied, as to *Anticipations* that if I only knew the amount of 'back' you *had* put into it, I should not etc. etc. Nevertheless, I still think you might advantageously have martyrised yourself a little more. The sexual chapter was very disappointing to me. It didn't seem to be thought out to a finish, and it seemed to say either not nearly enough or too much. If you had other things to say, not meant for England, I hope you will arrange to put them in full in the French edition. That chapter was full of unconvincingness for me. For example, the suggestion that 'adult' matter should, or could, be kept from the young by means of a high price, struck me as singularly inept. I do not see how it can stand up against criticism for a single instant. And it is a crucial point. Also your remarks on literature as such betray your fundamental inability to grasp what art is, really. The literary sense can*not* be quickened in the manner suggested at the bottom of p. 372.[1] If you could

---

[1] "A few carefully chosen pages of contemporary rubbish, read with a running comment, a few carefully chosen pages of what is,

only see how you give the show away by such a remark as that about Plato on p. 334![1] As a mere matter of opinion, my opinion is absolutely the reverse of yours that "every well-known living writer is or has been writing too much." Quite the contrary.

And in view of your terrific indictment of the English peoples for mauling the English language, I think the mere writing of a lot of the book falls short of even a respectable average. In *Anticipations* the sentences were over-loaded, and the words badly arranged, and often the meaning had to be disentangled. The same here, only more so. You have just got to face the fact that I was continually, except in the best passages, irritated by the bad technique of the writing. How do you defend this: "It is one of the most amazing aspects of contemporary life, to converse with some smart ... woman etc" (p. 164)? There were sundry examples of bad grammar, scores of bad punctuation, hundreds of striking inelegance, and not a few of an obscurity that might easily have been avoided. You may say that these things are nothing, that you can't be bothered with them; in the spirit which asks me whether I can't see the humour of advising the

---

comparatively, not rubbish, a little lucid discussion of effects and probabilities would do more to quicken the literary sense of the average person than all the sham enthusiasm about Marlowe and Spenser that was ever concocted."

[1] "Plato, for example, who has certainly in the very best translations quite perceptibly no greater mind than Lord Bacon, Newton, Darwin, or Adam Smith, becomes god-like to all who pass beyond the Little Go."

literary aspirant to begin with spelling. But it won't do, my son. And I half believe you jolly well know it. I sit at your feet in many things, but when I ope my mouth on the art and craft of your trade it behoves you to listen. There is a blind spot in your eye; either that or you are wayward. Now reread p. 1 of this present effusion.

I have got a "charming little flat" here, and furnished it myself. When next you run over to Switzerland for half a day, you must look in.

Best respex to the Mrs.

Yours

E. A. B.

I hope this letter will get through on $2\frac{1}{2}$d., but I have a sort of horrid doubt it will be overweight.

I am very happy to admit that that phrase "the artist living angrily in a stuffy little corner of pure technique," is an example of brilliant witty writing and perfectly just criticism. It amused me for hours.

50

WELLS TO BENNETT

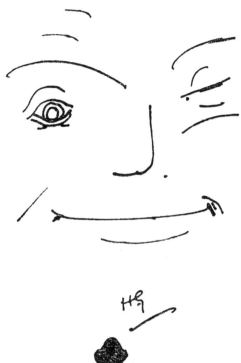

P. T.O

Spade House

Sandgate

[*October* 1903]

Really I have known most of what you say, but your
saying it will most certainly make me more heedful and

make it easier to be heedful of these slovenlinesses in future. And I'm just sending your *How to be &c* to a young man newly come to town from Cambridge, intending to write.

51

BENNETT TO WELLS

Hotel d'Italie

4 *January* 1904   *Menton*

DEAR ONES,

Your sweet note to hand. I have been here 20 days, and am writing a play with Phillpotts, which will be finished in a few days.[1] For my views, ideas, and sensations, see *T. P. cum grano*.[2] I do not expect to stay here after the end of next week, as my mother is disconcertingly ill and I am 2 days off London, where she is. I shall return to Paris. I only came to England for a few days at Xmas, and those few days I spent with her in the Five Towns, where I mingled in the great 'Vice' controversy with great pyrotechnic effect.[3] Just before leaving Paris I

[1] *A Credit to Human Nature*, never published or produced.

[2] Bennett at this time was writing a series of articles for *T.P.'s Weekly* entitled "A Novelist's Log Book." The series ran from 13 November 1903 to 11 May 1904.

[3] A Burslem parson, the Reverend Leonard Tyrwhitt, had denounced from the pulpit the excessive vice in the Potteries. His "crusade" was widely publicized, and Bennett, in a letter to the *Staffordshire Sentinel*, strenuously resisted Tyrwhitt's allegations, maintaining that vice was no more prevalent in the Potteries than in any other industrial district.

read the first instalment of *F. of G.*[1] in *Pearson's* and thought it extremely good, barring a few *minime* verbal infelicities. It cost me 2 francs to buy the number, but I couldn't resist it. I am now writing a humourous novel[2] — I don't know why, except that I wanted to, and there was a humourous story of mine in January *Windsor*[3] which the man who says is *not* humourous is a fool and no gentleman. Our play is marketable footle; hence I do not enlarge on it. Walking down Fleet Street the other day I was told you had yet another child.[4] My felicitations. I hope all are doing well. I wish you would come to Paris for a few days. So easy for you. I've got a nice little flat there, right in the middle, and give afternoon teas there with immense effect. I don't know when I shall live in England again. Are you going anywhere in the summer? I had meant to stay here till middle of March but see *ante*. When I have finished this humourous novel, I have four other novels waiting their turn. I have instructed them to form a queue and wait quietly. I take it you are going to revert next to *Love and Mr. L.* vein. I hope so. I had an evening with your Parisian impresario Kozaciewicz,[5] a few weeks ago, and found him decidedly

---

[1] *The Food of the Gods*, which ran in *Pearson's Magazine* from December 1903 to June 1904.   [2] *A Great Man*, May 1904.

[3] "His Worship the Goosedriver." Bennett notes in his *Journal* in January 1904, as warrant of his recent success, that the *Windsor* had commissioned him to do six stories.

[4] Frank Richard, born November 1903.

[5] B. Kozaciewicz, translator, with Henry Davray, of *Anticipations* into French.

intelligent, and interested sensibly in music too. These Parisian johnnies have a wonderfully just and clear-headed notion of you. You can't bounce them, you know. I suppose you *do* know. I do not think *Romance* [1] is good. In fact it isn't, and I don't care who knows it. Ever read Dostoevsky's *Crime and Punishment?* English translation damnable; but it is a *novel*. I'm just reading it again. I'm very keen on Monte Carlo at present. I've seldom been more interested in anything than I am in M.C.[2] Write and tell me you will come to Paris.

Yours ever

E. A. B.

52

WELLS TO BENNETT

Spade House

Sandgate

29 *March* 1904

DEAR OLD BENNETT

Wish I was coming to Paris, but I've got a damned book [3] in hand that necessitates reading all Plato and most other things if it is to be done properly and my poor dear nose is on the grindstone. Life keeps bright and

[1] A novel (1903) by Conrad in collaboration with Ford Madox Hueffer (later Ford). Wells thought very highly of it.

[2] Bennett made Henry Shakespeare Knight, his protagonist, in *A Great Man*, break the bank at Monte Carlo.

[3] *A Modern Utopia*, 1905.

everything goes well, but the Conrads are under an upset hay cart as usual, and God knows what is to be done.[1] J. C. ought to be administered by trustees.

Send me your comic novel to abuse.

Yours ever

H. G.

53

BENNETT TO WELLS [*Postcard*]

4 *Rue de Calais*

Tuesday [26 *April* 1904]   *Paris*

MY DEAR H. G.

Thanks for your letter. You seem detestably happy.

I have just given a letter of introduction to you to a man I know, Aleister Crowley, who (with his wife) is coming over to England tomorrow and is stopping the night at the Metropole, Folkestone, in order that he may

[1] In a letter to Wells dated 30 November 1903 Conrad had written "Things are bad with me—there's no disguising the fact. Not only is the scribbling awfully in arrears but there's no 'spring' in me to grapple with it effectually. Formerly, in my sea life, a difficulty nerved me to the effort; now I perceive it is not so. However don't imagine I've given up, but there is an uncomfortable sense of losing my footing in deep waters." In a letter to David S. Meldrum on 5 April 1904, Conrad writes of his fear that his wife is to be a helpless cripple as the result of a fall, of his own physical and mental debilities and his financial difficulties. (*Joseph Conrad: Letters to William Blackwood and David S. Meldrum*, ed. by William Blackburn, 1958.)

call on you; he wants to ask your opinion about *Time*.[1]
He is a poet of some parts, and a really considerable
traveller. I expect he will call on you Thursday. Beneath
his eastern exterior there is something in him.

Love to the darlings, and homage to their mamma.

Thine

E. A. B.

54

WELLS TO BENNETT

Spade House

29 *April* 1904   Sandgate

MY DEAR E. A. B.

No little friends of yours have turned up. But I shall
be very glad to see anyone fresh from your benedictions
and still more pleased to see yourself. Let me know
when you are about.

Yours ever

H. G.

---

[1] Crowley was the founder of a mystic, atheistic organization
that had such tenets as "the law of the strong: this is our law and the
joy of the world" and "Do what thou wilt shall be the whole of the
law." Crowley later sent Wells an admission card to the "Rite of
Jupiter" held by his organization.

55

WELLS TO BENNETT

20 *May* 1904   *Sandgate*

DEAR OLD E. A. B.

You shouldn't call a book "A Frolic" [1]—it's young—but the book *is* a frolic and a very good one. You don't know quite how well you can do this sort of thing and consequently you don't do it quite so well as you could—you hurry out of it at last. For all that it's first-rate and human and with something personal and distinctive that *Leonora* lacked. I wish it was longer, and with more about Geraldine, who's dashed in something reckless. I wonder if you had planned it more whether it would have been better or worse. It might have bit a little more I think. It's a success at Spade House, but I think it will be a lot too short and not complicated enough for the Beast.[2] I'd congratulate most men I know on this book. As for congratulating *you*—I don't know. I think you might have done it better.

Yours ever

H. G.

[1] Bennett's *A Great Man, A Frolic* (1904).
[2] In Wells's correspondence "the Beast" means either an editor or the reading public.

56

BENNETT TO WELLS

4 *Rue de Calais*

25 *May* 1904   *Paris*

MY DEAR H. G.

Much touched. My only surprise is you don't find
more fault with it. As a matter of fact, I could have done
it better, especially towards the end. But, having conceived it as a 'lark,' I fell into the error of regarding it
technically as a 'lark' also. One writing. No draft.
Practically no erasures, and about two months' work at
most. But then you always prefer the work which costs
one the least trouble. Now *Leonora*,—but what is the
use of talking about colours to the blind? And that reminds me that your last *Strand* story was really admirable.[1] A little faint towards the end I thought, but
fundamentally *damn good*. Strangely enough, though I
never met anyone who perceived the satiric quality in
The First Men in the Moon, I have met several who
have spontaneously explained to me that the *Strand*
story is a "fine criticism of life." After this handsome
praise, if you should come across a story of mine in the

[1] "The Country of the Blind," April 1904.

May *Windsor* [1] the least you can do is think it very good.

I must see you in the summer.

Yours ever

E. A. B.

57

BENNETT TO WELLS

4 Rue de Calais

27 September 1904　　　　　　　　　　　　*Paris*

MY DEAR H. G.

I am disposed to agree with your own estimate of "Scepticism of the Instrument." [2] I don't, however, think that your third indictment of the instrument is quite new. At any rate it is one which I have often formulated (clumsily) to myself.[3] I wish I was a "scientific thinker," so that my praise of your brief but startling opusculum might carry more weight. I have had no

[1] "Nocturne at the Majestic."

[2] A paper read by Wells to the Oxford Philosophical Society on 8 November 1903, and published as an appendix to *A Modern Utopia*.

[3] The "instrument" in question here is the generally accepted logical process of thought. Wells's third indictment of this process is the tendency of logicians to use the same terms for different "planes" or circumstances. Thus the "universe at that plane to which the mind of the molecular physicist descends has none of the shapes or forms of our common life whatever." (*A Modern Utopia*, 1905, p. 388.)

opportunity till now of writing you, and I only write now because I want information from you. Outside the N. L. C.,[1] what Clubs do you belong to? I want to belong to a club (not the N. L. C.) where I can have a bedroom when I want it; I am going to chuck the flat. What do you suggest? Do you belong to the Savile? I rather think Marriott Watson is a pillar of that. Kindly put your back into this club-question, as it is now important for me. I write to you because you look on clubs with a fresh and unbiassed eye.

Respex to Madame
Your
E. A. B.

P. S. Ignore my next book.[2] It is naught.

58

BENNETT TO WELLS

2 *October* 1904

4 *Rue de Calais*
Paris

MY DEAR H. G.

Many thanks. The Royal Societies is clearly my club. But is it not confined to members of learned societies? Should I have to get into some learned society first? Kindly oblige me further by informing me as to this and telling me of anyone whom you know or I know who is a member.

[1] National Liberal Club.   [2] *Teresa of Watling Street.*

When I said that *Teresa of Watling St.* was no good, I
meant that it was *really* no good.   Still you shall see it.   I
am an excellent judge of my own work.   I have got influenza, and was reading *Anna >5 T∧* tonight.   It is a
masterpiece.   I see that clearly.   Before reading *Anna* I
re-read *The Sleeper.*   Your opinion of that book is wrong.
It is a *fine* work.   All that it lacks is a little more absence of
strenuousness.   I read it clean through at two sittings:
That is the highest praise any work can have.   Ask
Davray if I am not a good judge of my own work.   By
the way, who the hell is M. Blunt?[1]   Is it Davray?[2]   I
think M. Blunt is apt to lay down canons for English that
English won't have, but you know that on the whole I am
a pro-Blunt.   It is only because I have reasons for not
wanting to quarrel with you that I have refrained from
joining the "W. G." correspondence,[3] and really showing

[1] In the September 1904 issue of *La Nouvelle Revue* appeared
an article by Frank Blunt entitled "*M. H.-G. Wells et le Style.*"
Blunt complains that Wells writes "*au courant de la plume*" and has
no regard for the refinements of writing.   As proof, Blunt examines
individual passages and pages of *Place aux Géants* (*The Food of the
Gods*) and points out numerous repetitions of individual words and
monotonies of pattern.   He maintains that these defects of Wells's
prose are corrected by his French translators.

[2] Henry D. Davray, French translator of Wells's *The Island
of Dr. Moreau* and, with B. Kozakiewicz, *Anticipations.*   He was
also a member of the staff of the *Mercure de France* as director of
the section on foreign publications.

[3] The *Westminster Gazette.*   In a review of Wells's *Food of the
Gods* in the November 1904 issue of the *Mercure de France*, Davray
refers to the stir created in England by Blunt's article in *La Nouvelle Revue: "A peine arrivé sur le sol britannique, je tombai dans le*

H

you up. I have a collection of your sins that would end the matter once for all so far as you are concerned. However, in practising the higher literary carelessness you are merely following the example of most English great writers. You are no worse than Scott, Dickens, Thackeray, and the Brontës, and you are a jolly sight better than Jane Austen. Don't forget to cause *The Food of the Gods* to be sent to me. I wish I hadn't read it, so that I could read it again for the first time. My "heresy" articles in *T. P.s Weekly* have raised a devil of a dust.[1] Eden [2] is very sick because I have ignored Blackmore, and the Tennysonians are furious. "T. P." is angry, and Whitten says he made a mistake in asking me to write the articles. What a world! Kindly tell Davray I am expecting to hear from him with an appointment to meet him and Madame as they pass through Paris. They must come here for tea.

Love to all

E. A. B.

---

plus profond ahurissement: dans un grand nombre de journaux, la polémique faisait rage autour de cet article." Davray dismisses Blunt's criticism rather contemptuously, saying that one should not take seriously the fantasies of a facetious critic who resorts to arithmetic to find fault with an author whom he pretends to admire.

[1] Bennett had been writing a series of articles in *T.P.'s Weekly* entitled "My Literary Heresies," in which he calls Tennyson a minor poet. The series ran from 9 September 1904 to 23 September 1904.

[2] Eden Phillpotts.

59

WELLS TO BENNETT

Spade House

3 *October* 1904   *Sandgate*

MY DEAR BENNETT.

It is not at all difficult to join a Royal Society if that is necessary for that club—but is it? The Secretary will tell you. M. Blunt—Davray says—is the hireling of a Jew enemy. Stile [1] my dear chap in this sense of a petty word mongering has no place in English literature. The stile of my general design, the stile of my thought—C'est moi! I don't care a bit if you write about my stile—you will do me honour—provided always that you make it insistently clear that in this matter I am at one with all the English swells. The only thing I fear and which makes me sore is the sort of criticism that checks the expanding common reviewer, chills Macmillan's advertisement imbecile, and delays my getting audible. I am honestly doing what I can to clear my prose of repetition and so on, but except among passages of high value I don't see the force of writing for beauty of phrase. See?

---

[1] An intentional misspelling. Wells is carrying on the little joke he began in letter 48 with reference to Bennett's *How To Become an Author*.

The Davrays send their love and Vallée[1] also—
joining therein with us.

Yours ever

H. G.

60

BENNETT TO WELLS

4 *Rue de Calais*

7 *February* 1905   [*Paris*]

MY DEAR H. G.

I am much refreshed and encouraged. And I need it,
as I have got stuck in the middle of my magnificent new
novel [2]—chiefly owing to a bad attack of influenza.

Surely the irony of my descriptions of leading hotels is
not too fine for you! "Tiddy fol-lol" is not good, as sich,
but seeing that I wrote it for *Lloyds Newspaper* and that it
appeared there, it is astoundingly good. However, I
doubt if it should have appeared in the book.[3]

As to Eden, much may be said on your side, but I
think you are constitutionally incapable (artistically too

---

[1] Probably Dr Vallée, Bennett's physician at Les Sablons and a
mutual friend of Bennett and Davray.

[2] *Sacred and Profane Love.*

[3] *Tales of the Five Towns*, January 1905. "Tiddy-Fol-Lol" is a
slight story of the reconciliation of an estranged father and daughter.
Some of the stories in *Tales of the Five Towns* have large hotels as
their setting, i.e., "Nocturne at the Majestic."

irritable and too much preoccupied with mere ideas) to appreciate what really is fine, classical, and indeed great in *The Secret Woman*.[1] The whole book is far finer than any part of it. However. . . .

Hommages à Madame

Yours

E. A. B.

Why in Hades do you let Pinker put stuff like your old burglary story in *Pearson's Mag.* as new work?[2] The money isn't worth it.

61

BENNETT TO WELLS

4 *Rue de Calais*

18 *April* 1905 [*Paris*]

MY DEAR H. G.

Many thanks for the book.[3] If it was a novel I could say something useful about it, but as it isn't, I don't

---

[1] Eden Phillpotts's *The Secret Woman*, 1905.

[2] "The Hammerpound Park Burglary," June 1905. The story had previously appeared as the thirteenth in *The Stolen Bacillus and Others*, November 1895. But in the December 1904 issue of *Pearson's* the editors had appended to Wells's "A Moth-Genus Nova," which had appeared as the fourteenth story in *The Stolen Bacillus*, a statement that this and some stories in future issues had already appeared in book form but were being reprinted to give them a wider audience.

[3] *A Modern Utopia*, 1905.

know that I can. The latter half of it is much more convincing and suggestive than the first half, and is also better done, but all of it is better than *Mankind in the Making*. The two things that strike me about the whole thing are the enormous difficulties you have had to face, and the continuous brainwork that there is in it. It is a book that deserves to be called "gallant." Of course what interests me most, and what will interest everyone most, is your development of the hierarchy idea. When I read your opening sentences about the Samurai I thought the section was fanciful and impossible, but I was gradually convinced of its possibility. I see that some people are grumbling at you because such a caste would do a great deal of harm. But that is not the point. The point is whether such a caste will come into existence. It might. I think it would work first good and then harm, like most institutions. But anyhow you have handled it most fearfully well. It sticks in my mind. It is astonishing to me that a man of your imagination, so untrammeled as it is, my poor boy, should be capable of the attitude toward the Hampstead middle class disclosed on p. 56. This is one of your class-prejudices and you can't leave it alone. But you surely must see that what produces the Hampstead middle class will exist in no matter what Utopia. It is a relative matter. Relatively, the Hampstead middle class is a fine achievement of human progress; and relatively it is also the despicable thing you insist on rendering it. Your attitude to it is not that of a philosopher but that of a Chelsea painter who has not 'arrived' and sits drinking at the Six Bells while cursing all Philistines and plutocrats.

You are very good about women. I liked all that. Personally, my ideas are more oriental, but still there are times when I am not oriental. What you say about the ugliness of modern women's dress is absolutely wrong. Indeed your notions about material beauty are shockingly inferior to your other notions. You would like to laugh me out of being a Cultivated Person, but you never will, and as a Cultivated Person I say that your remarks on architecture, for example, are painful. And yet you *have* a glimmering, sometimes, even about architecture. It is most extraordinary how, immediately you come to the region of moral ideas, your language becomes distinguished. "The intricate, austere, and courageous imagination of our race" is admirably said. Your analysis of political parties in England fills me with awe. It is A 1, and the indictment of Liberalism is excellent—though I *am* a Liberal, like yourself. There is something about the precocity of civilisation on p. 292 that also is worthy of you. But why should the Samurai have any religion? I hope you aren't going to defend that worn out platitude to the effect that religion is a necessity of man's nature. Because it isn't. Religion is done for—any sort of religion. Your notions of a religion for the Samurai startled me.

The botanist is bitterly and well done. You have got

him and all his tribe perfectly on p. 232.[1] And I think he serves his purpose very well in the book. I wouldn't like to pronounce offhand as to the success of the mere literary machinery of the book. But I rather fancy at present that you have succeeded in spite of it. I would respectfully point out that in the italicised prologue you have most definitely visualised the voice as a person on a platform at a cinematograph show, while in the italicised epilogue he is 'carried onward' through the streets. Arthur Balfour might dialectically defend this, but it is a little confusing. Sullivan's illustrations are not as good as the others he did for you. They show a notable falling-off—not in conception but in execution.

You understand, my attitude toward this book is very humble. I could only authoritatively find fault with its grammar. It has much impressed me, and some of its things stick brilliantly in my mind. Kindest regards to you both.

Yours

E. A. B.

[1] "Now the botanist's imagination is always busy with the most impossible make-believe. . . . It may be he is essentially different from me, but I am much more inclined to think he is simply more childish. Always it is make believe. He believes that horses are beautiful creatures for example, dogs are beautiful creatures, that some women are inexpressively lovely, and he makes believe that this is always so. . . . Then there is his botany. He makes believe that all the vegetable kingdom is mystically perfect and exemplary, that all flowers smell deliciously and are exquisitely beautiful. . . . But I know, and I am querulously incapable of understanding why

62

WELLS TO BENNETT

Spade House
Sandgate

25 *September* 1905

DEAR BENNETT.

It *is* good and it *is* bad, and it is most interesting and readable.[1] Ouida and the best French models and our Bennett and a certain extraordinary and persistent cleverness take me in gusts. Your English though is much less clear and simple than it was—stresses on the epithets, and a surface of hard bright points. And I feel more than ever the difference between our minds. You are always taking surface values that I reject, hotels are not luxurious, *trains de luxe* are full of coal grit, *chefs* and pianists are not marvellous persons, dramatic triumphs are silly uproars. But it isn't irony—you believe in these things. There never was a woman like your woman, but no end of women journalists and minor actresses have imagined

---

everyone else does not know, that a horse is beautiful in one way and quite ugly in another, that everything has this shot-silk quality, and is all the finer for that. . . . There is indeed no beauty whatever save that transitory thing that comes and comes again; all beauty is really the beauty of expression, is really kinetic and momentary." (*A Modern Utopia*, 1905.) The botanist is a foil to the Owner of the Voice, the "I" of this passage, and, we can safely assume, Wells himself.

[1] *Sacred and Profane Love*, 1905.

themselves like her. For some unfathomable reason you don't penetrate. You are like George Moore. You have probably never been in love. I doubt if ever you weep. You have no passion for Justice. You prefer 'style' to beauty. You are not a poet, you are not a genius. But you are a dear delightful person and please let me know what time you come to England.

Yours ever

H. G.

63

BENNETT TO WELLS

4 Rue de Calais

30 *September* 1905   *Paris*

MY DEAR WELLS

Amid the chorus ("a great book, a great book") which that glittering novel has naturally called forth from most of my friends, your letter, with its thin small handwriting, is like a grandma announcing that I have been having too much sugar in my tea and must be content with half a lump. My dear H. G. you move me to explain myself to you. I have not yet decided whether I am a genius, but I shall probably decide, with that astounding quality of self-criticism that I have, that I am not. I am probably too clever, and, what is more important, too infernally well-balanced. I am ready to agree with you that no such woman as Carlotta ever existed. No character in any novel is more than a hint at the real thing, and it is right it should be so. You can't honestly say that Mr. Lewisham ever existed. You know, we all know, that after all our satisfaction with Mr. Lewisham, he never lived and couldn't have lived. He is an arrangement to suit the necessities of a convention; and here and there he bears a resemblance to a man. I choose Mr. Lewisham because he is one of the least unreal characters I can recall at the moment. All I would claim for Carlotta is that now and then she does what a real woman would do, and that her stiff lay-figure movements are sometimes really not so very stiff. Again, I must agree with you as to the style. But incidentally you must remember that this is not my style, but Carlotta's style, and that it cost me a Hades of a lot of trouble. I am inclined to think however that as regards style the best book I ever wrote was *A Man from the North*. The question of my style must really be looked into. I have never been in love. Sometimes the tears start to my eyes, but they never fall. These things are indubitable. I have no passion for Justice. That also is profoundly true. I recognise that progress is inevitable and that it can only be achieved by a passion for justice. But I reckon I am above a passion for justice. There we come to "the difference between our minds." I look down from a height on the show and contemplate a passion for justice much as I contemplate the other ingredients.

Whereas you are simply a passion for justice incarnate. You aren't an artist, except insofar as you disdainfully make use of art for your reforming ends; you are simply a reformer—with the classic qualities of the reformer. Hence your amazing judgments on Balzac, Milton, etc. Like all great reformers you are inhuman, and scornful of everything that doesn't interest you. Hence the complaint of the anti-Wellsites that in your "scientific" novels, there is no individual interest, that the characters don't exist individually. A not unjust complaint. The pity is that these persons cannot perceive the "concerted" interest of your "scientific" novels. You are not really interested in individual humanity. And when you write a "non-scientific" novel, you always recur to a variation of the same type of hero, and you always will, because your curiosity about individualities won't lead you further. You are concerned in big crowd-movements. Art, really, you hate. It means to you what "arty" means to me. You live in a nice house, but you know perfectly well you wouldn't care what sort of a house you lived in. When you say that a great pianist is not a marvellous person, you give the show away. For you he is not. The astounding human interest of a dramatic triumph is for you a "silly uproar." In these two instances you show clearly, as regards art and as regards life, where your interests stop. You won't have anything to do with "surface values" at all. You don't merely put them in a minor place; you reject them. A

couple of pages devoted to surface values will irritate you.
You will never see it, but in rejecting surface values you
are wrong. As a fact they are just as important as other
values. But reformers can't perceive this. They are
capable of classing chefs, pianists and *trains de luxe* all
together and saying: "Go to, I am a serious person."
You are, you know. The same spirit animates you as
animated George Macdonald's grandmother, who ob-
jected to the violin as a profane instrument. And the
mischief is that, though you will undoubtedly do a vast
amount of good in the world, you will get worse and
worse, more and more specialised, more and more scornful. All this is not an explanation of you; but an explanation of me. It "connotes" the difference between
our minds. I proposed writing to you to offer Mrs.
Wells and you the advantage of my presence for a night
or so on my way to England early in December. If this
suits, I can then respectfully listen to your defence. I am
much too vain to mind being called "not a poet," and
"not a genius." But to be called a "dear delightful
person" rouses my worst instincts. It makes me feel as if
I was like Marriott Watson or Pett Ridge,[1] and I ain't,
not really.

Hommages à Madame
Thine
E. A. B.

[1] William Pett Ridge, a prolific writer of popular novels. He
published steadily until his death in 1930.

64

WELLS TO BENNETT

Spade House

[*October* 1905]   *Sandgate*

DEAR BENNETT

You're a good upstanding person. All I've said was right but I like your spirit. We shall look forward to Dec. when your education will be resumed.

Yours ever,

H. G.

65

BENNETT TO WELLS

4 *Rue de Calais*

9 *November* 1905   [Paris]

MY DEAR H. G.,

The only real seizable fault that I can find in *Kipps* [1] is the engagement to Helen, which entirely failed to convince me. In fact it is useless to tell me they ever were engaged. I do not believe it. If you had made of Helen a less real and lifelike figure than she is, then I might have been persuadable. But she is extremely well done, and so she gives you the lie in the matter of the engagement.

[1] 1905.

Ann is more than well-done, she is Very Fine, and the Ann scenes are the best in the book. After agreeing with myself that I read the thing all through with eagerness and joy, and after telling myself that I must not expect in your 'human interest' novels those aspects of life which you either can't see or disdain to see, I find myself asking what this book "proves", and not getting any answer.[1] As it is distinctly a fighting, '*tendencieux*' book, I think I ought to have an answer. Why this immense animus against the "nace"[2] class of person, since we are all human together? Am I to understand that in your opinion as a purposeful observer of life the 'nace' class is more ridiculous, or less worthy of sympathy, or less the outcome of natural and inevitable causes, than any other class? I ask for information. I don't think your ferocious hostility to about five sixths of the characters in the book makes for righteousness of any kind, and certainly not for artistic righteousness. Especially as you follow Kipps about on the stage with a rose-coloured lime light. What is the theory of this procedure? There is no doubt that you achieve the illusion of reality in spite of it, and not with its aid.

[1] In a *Journal* entry for 7 November 1905 Bennett writes, "I have just finished reading [Zola's] *L'Œuvre*. It has taken me a long time, because I left it in the middle to read Wells's *Kipps*. What a colossal affair it seems by the side of *Kipps*, so serious, tremendous and imposing." (I, 222.)

[2] Mr Chester Coote's pronunciation of "nice." Coote is Kipps's chaperon into "the higher and better sort of English life."

If you have set out to amuse and divert the B.P. you have richly succeeded in your aim. Ditto if you have tried to enlist their sympathies on behalf of the Kippses and the Anns. Ditto if you have tried to give impartial portraits of the Sids, the Mastermans and the Chitterlows. But if you have had any Larger aim, any aim of showing how and why one class of persons generally is superior or inferior to another, then I don't reckon you have succeeded—at any rate with thoughtful, judicious, and high-minded people like myself, Mr. Popple (if his name *is* Popple), and others. You said last year, you even faithfully promised, that you were going to write with more care. God-a-mercy! After the sentence on p. 409 beginning: "Next to starting a haberdasher's shop," I renounce the crusade.[1] I respectfully give you up. Damn it, after all it doesn't matter how you write. But after your animadversions on the Head Master of Dulwich. . . .! By the way your *Westminster Gazette* article [2] was magnificent, and filled me with holy joy.

I have a sort of idea that my objections to *Kipps* (except as to the engagement) are rather vague and 'theoretical.' But nevertheless I think they contain food

[1] The entire sentence is "Next to starting a haberdasher's shop, I doubt if Kipps could have been more truly happy than during the weeks of preparation."

[2] "The Schoolmaster and the Empire," 21 October 1905, later published as the sixteenth paper of *An Englishman Looks at the World*, 1914. In the article Wells attacks an essay, "English Ideas on Education," by the Headmaster of Dulwich, appearing in the *Independent Review*.

for your thought. Such is my view. That there is "a laugh on every page" is beside the point.

I trust to present my respects in person to Madame in about a month's time.

Yours ever,
E. A. B.

66

BENNETT TO WELLS

4 Rue de Calais

1 *December* 1905   [*Paris*]

MY DEAR H. G.

Monday week is the 11th. Suppose I arrive on that night at my usual hour and derive advantage from you and Madame for 36 hours? Will this suit her and you?

Yours
E. A. B.

67

BENNETT TO MRS WELLS

31, Spencer Road

Saturday [16 *December* 1905]   *Putney S.W.*

DEAR MRS. WELLS,

I suppose you knew all the time that that train didn't go near St. Paul's or Holborn. It went to Cannon St. and

I

arrived in nice time for afternoon tea. Thanks to your admirable sandwiches, however, I suffered no discomfort, except from cold feet. What a line! In spite of the line being what it is, I would never, in your place, leave your house. In a word, you are misguiding yourselves in going to London. You will regret it, and what is more important, I shall. I shall have no place to call at, and be looked after, and be fed up with world-theories and the greatest music. In fact I shall take the cheap route, Southampton, and generally descend in the scale of things. Kindly think over this prospect, and remember me to Gyp, Frank,[1] their author, and the pianola.

A merry Xmas
Yours sincerely
E. A. BENNETT

P.S. And a happy new year, but I hope you won't sell your house.

68

WELLS TO BENNETT

Spade House

3 *February* 1906   *Sandgate*

MY DEAR BENNETT.

It's all yours is *Hugo* [2]—and nobody but you could have done it. It's grandio-Bennett-esque, it is magnified

---

[1] Wells's sons, George Philip and Frank.
[2] *Hugo, A Fantasia on Modern Themes*, 1906.

and distorted and glittering and absurd and we like it no end.

We rejoice in you and salute you.

We, poor souls, are torn apart in April and I go to America to write articles and see.

Yours ever

H. G.

69

BENNETT TO WELLS

Les Sablons [1]

près Moret

S & M

France

29 *June* 1906 [postmark]

MY DEAR WELLS,

I meant to reply to your last letter, and then I waited for your return from U.S. and now I see the announcement of your articles in the *Tribune* [2] and I sat down at once,—to tell you and your wife that I am engaged to be married to a young woman of the name of Eléanora Green, a native of Savannah, Georgia, who has lived nearly all her life in Paris. Her age is 25. I can't tell you

[1] Bennett maintained an apartment here for periodic visits. It was in the house of a couple named Lebert, retired after thirty-one years of railway work in Paris, whose recollections of the Commune Bennett was to use in *The Old Wives' Tale*.

[2] The *Tribune*, published in London. The series of articles later appeared as *The Future in America, A Search After Realities*, 1906.

any more about her (except that she was destined for an operatic singer, and I stepped in just in time to stop her debut), because I don't know any more. Let us see what kind of a letter of congratulation a publicist and a professional penman can write under these circumstances.

Love to you both

E. A. BENNETT

P.S. How are you both?

70

BENNETT TO WELLS

4 Rue de Calais

Tuesday [*July* 1906]   [*Paris*]

MY DEAR H. G.

Your letter had an immense success with my girl. She has a passion for stern realism. I read her parts of it. Your Chicago article was very good. All that you say about marriage and Chicago is true. And as for your and your wife's good wishes, they give me joy.

I am—I mean we are—thinking of being married at a registry office in Folkestone, this being handiest. If you are summering in Sandgate, I wonder if you will let me accomplish a formal residence at your house. It means 2 days at the beginning of the legal term of 16 days, and then another two days at the end—four days in all. Continuous residence is not necessary. Will this worry you?

It would occur in August *about* the 8th to 10th and 22nd to 24th. The marriage will not take place till October. Have no apprehension as to being worried in any way by the actual marriage. You will neither see nor hear anything of it. Eléanora will bring one friend over with her for a night, and the other witness I will get in the registry office.

I see you are turning the Fabian inside out?[1]

Yours ever

E. A. B.

71

BENNETT TO WELLS

Eltham

Torquay

[*July* 1906]

MY DEAR H. G.

Many thanks for your note. I will take my chance. In fact I must do, as I *have* no dates at present. I'll write

---

[1] Wells joined the Fabian Society in 1903. In February 1906 he read a paper, "The Faults of the Fabian," which called for drastic alterations in the organization and programme of the group. For months he led a small revolt against the control of "the Old Gang" —Mr and Mrs Bernard Shaw, Sidney and Beatrice Webb, and others. Several of his suggestions were adopted, but after a year of various committee meetings, reports and answers to reports, he was easily outmanoeuvred by Shaw. He wrote of it in his *Experiment in Autobiography*, "No part of my career rankles so acutely in my memory with the conviction of bad judgment, gusty impulse and real inexcusable vanity, as that storm in the Fabian tea-cup." (II, 660.)

later on. My address from Wednesday will be Duchy House, Princetown, Dartmoor. I'm going up there with Eden [1] to fix up a new collaborated serial, the last having been a marked success.[2] Your U.S.A. articles are going on excellently.

I'm going on pretty well.

Ever yours

E. A. B.

72

BENNETT TO WELLS

4 Rue de Calais

Saturday [4 *August* 1906]   [*Paris*]

MY DEAR H. G.

I shall not come next Wednesday. My engagement exists no longer.[3] Can't write to you about it now, but it's right bang off, anyhow. I shall hope to come later on, if you will have me for a day or two.

Yours ever

E. A. B.

[1] Eden Phillpotts.

[2] *The Sinews of War, A Romance of London and the Sea,* 1906.

[3] According to Pound, Eleanora Green had never taken Bennett's proposal seriously. She looked upon him as a likeable but essentially avuncular, middle-aged person. She was, by her testimony, completely unaware of Bennett's preparations for their marriage, having not even bothered to read his letters. When she realised the seriousness of his intentions, she broke the engagement.

73

BENNETT TO WELLS

4 *Rue de Calais*
7 *September* 1906   [*Paris*]

MY DEAR H. G.

I had to leave England all of a sudden, and I am going to Holland tomorrow to stay with some friends. As, however, I cannot deprive myself of your Light, I propose to come over for a week-end sometime next month. Five hours will see me at your place. I shall just go no further than Sandgate. I will write later to consult your august convenience. You both flourish, naturally.

Yours ever,
E. A. B.

74

WELLS TO BENNETT

Spade House
8 *September* 1906   *Sandgate*

DEAR BENNETT.

Where are you? Come and bring your bandaged Heart and sit down here for a day or so beside my bandaged knee (I've sprained it badly). House is clear—

except for one lady of unaggressive qualities—next week after Toosday. We *was* going to Switzerland. Incidentally I want to make you a Socialist.

Yours ever

H. G.

75

WELLS TO BENNETT

Spade House

[10 *September* 1906]   *Sandgate*

DEAR BENNETT

Why these secret comings and goings? What are you up to and how long are you in England for?

Your devoted

H. G.

76

BENNETT TO WELLS

Le Grand Hotel-Bruxelles

Monday [16 *September* 1906]   *Boulevard Anspach*

[*Brussels*]

MY DEAR WELLS

I have been yachting with anti-socialists in Holland and had no address for a week. Your two letters have just arrived at my bedside. So I can't come the day before yesterday. But I mean to come soon. You will find it

impossible to make me a socialist, as I already am one.
See?

I write you again soon.

What price Bart Kennedy[1] on America in the *Daily
Mail*? You are simply nowhere compared with his
grandiosity. Which reminds me that the title I had
chosen for my new book was discovered, at the last moment, to have been used by Fergus Hume[2] in 1891.
Fergus, on being applied to, as a matter of courtesy, for
permission to re-use the title, replied pompously that he
would have been delighted to accord the grace, had he
not recently granted a similar application from William
Le Queux!!

Wednesday I return to Paris,

Hommages à Madame

Yours ever

BENNETT

---

[1] London author and journalist, later editor of *Bart Kennedy's
Paper*, in which Wells held a small number of shares, and in 1926
editor of *Bart's Broadsheet* in Brighton.

[2] 1859–1932. Author of the extremely popular detective story,
The Mystery of a Hansom Cab, 1887. Hume eventually granted the
request, since Bennett's "new book" was published with the same
title as Hume's *Whom God Hath Joined*, 1891.

77

BENNETT TO WELLS

4 *Rue de Calais*

Friday [*September* 1906]   [*Paris*]

MY DEAR H. G.

Many thanks for the book,[1] which I found on my return from Holland yesterday. I have already given you my views at large on it. I was in the Paris office of the *Daily Express* last night, and was shown your slaughtering of them. These reviews, though ineffably stupid and somewhat dishonest, were inevitable. And I take it that, had it not been for your new socialistic prominence,[2] you would have received them with silence. But now you feel that the Cause is involved. Well, in your place, I should still be inclined to pursue a policy of masterly silence. The people who matter perfectly understand. And you will never persuade the people who don't matter that the close of the *Comet* is not profoundly immoral.

---

[1] *In the Days of the Comet*, 1906.

[2] In 1906 Wells had also published *The Faults of the Fabian* and *Socialism and the Family*. The controversy Bennett refers to concerns the reaction of the English press to what it interpreted as Wells's advocacy of free love in the last part of *In the Days of the Comet*. See, for instance, the review in *The Times Literary Supplement* of 17 September 1906, and Wells's answer on 28 September.

Such is my notion. And I think you honoured the
Express far too much by slaughtering it.

See you soon,

Yours

E. A. B.

P.S. This is quite private, and I would not be fair to the
Paris staff of the *Express* if it got about through me: they
were charmed to see the smashing. I don't think anyone
has a lower opinion of the *Express–Mail* type of paper
than the staffs thereof.

78

WELLS TO BENNETT

Spade House

27 November 1906   *Sandgate*

MY DEAR BENNETT,

   Whom God hath Joined is really a most extraordinary
good novel, full of knowledge and deft handling and a
loving sense of social situation. I'm damned if there
aren't too many good books altogether this year! There's
a dozen books at least which would have made a memorable season in the mournful old Victorian times, yours,[1]
mine (2),[2] Newbolt's quite charming book,[3] Doyle's *Sir*

---

[1] *Whom God Hath Joined*, 1906.
[2] *In the Days of the Comet* and *The Future in America*.
[3] Sir Henry Newbolt, *The Old Country*.

Nigel (really a most admirable piece of genre), Conrad's *The Mirror of the Sea*, Low's book on India.[1] *Whom God Hath Joined* I think I like best of all your work. It's a thousand miles better than *Sacred and Profane Copulation* and I really think more human than *A Great Man*.

Yours ever

H. G.

79

BENNETT TO WELLS

3 *Rue d'Aumale*

14 *December* 1906   [*Paris*]

MY DEAR H. G.,

I happened to meet Davray today. He told me you had declined an offer of a conference and a banquet here. I had not time to discuss it with him, but I gathered the refusal is because you are too busy. I didn't tell Davray that I should write to you, but I instantly decided to permit myself to meddle in your affairs to that extent. In my opinion if you do definitely refuse this thing you will make a great mistake—that is, if you care 2d. for renown and influence in France. I know all about the enterprise. It is under the very finest auspices in France, and has the active support of the very cream of the French Academy.

[1] Sir Sidney Low, *A Vision of India*.

A greater honour couldn't be offered to an English author. It is true they did it for Gosse; but that was a quid pro quo, in return for laudations rendered by him during many years in the English press. With you there can be no interested motive on their part. You cannot possibly be too busy to attend to a thing of this kind. If you don't accept it, it will be because you have not realised the genuineness of its importance. But you may take that from me, and most seriously. The thing is no affair of mine, but I should have something on my conscience if I didn't tell you that your refusal would amount to a crime against yourself.

Yours ever,

E. A. B.

80

WELLS TO BENNETT

Spade House

[*December* 1906]   *Sandgate*

MY DEAR BENNETT.

Now you realize my Greatness. Blow the French Academy!

Yours ever

H. G.

81

WELLS TO BENNETT

Spade House

20 *March* 1907   *Sandgate*

DEAR ARNOLD

You have produced a book *worthy* of the same covers as *Socialism and the Family*.[1] Rejoice!

Yours ever

H. G.

82

WELLS TO BENNETT

National Liberal Club

Saturday [June 1907]   *Whitehall Place, S.W.*

MY DEAR BENNETT.

So you *will* marry![2] Well, I've warned you once. Won't you come and see us for just a last dip before you change?

[1] Wells is referring to Bennett's *The Reasonable Life, Being Hints for Men and Women*, 1907, later expanded and re-published as *Mental Efficiency, and Other Hints to Men and Women*, 1911. Wells's *Socialism and the Family* had appeared in 1906. A. C. Fifield published both works.

[2] Bennett was to marry Marguerite Soulié on 4 July 1907. The daughter of a baker of Nègrepelisse, she had come to Paris to work for an aunt who owned a dressmaking establishment, and had

The Grim Smile [1] is I think your high watermark so far. I've read it and admire and envy a pen wonderfully under control and now astonishingly expert—I regret dissolute years. You get in now nearly all your natural liveliness of invention and humour. Never before have you got 50% of that.

Yours ever

H. G.

Warmest good wishes for the great experiment.

83

BENNETT TO WELLS

3 Rue d'Aumale

1 *July* 1907   [*Paris*]

MY DEAR H. G.

I had to come back to Paris by telegram, to arrange legal formalities for the accursed union. No end of trouble. However, I expect to be ruined artistically within a week from now, and all your warnings will have been in vain. I am extremely glad that you class *The Grim Smile*

---

some social success with recitals of the poems of Baudelaire and Verlaine. "'It is easy enough to understand what attracted him to his future wife,' says Georges Lafourcade: 'as a man, her beauty and personality; as an artist, her talent; as a native of the Five Towns, her Parisian characteristics; as a practical man, her domestic assets.'" (Pound, p. 176.)

[1] *The Grim Smile of the Five Towns*, 1907, a collection of short stories.

so high, though it shows a failure on your part to appreciate things like *Leonora*. Still, I am very content. I suppose I shall see you both sometime.

Kindest regards to your wife,

Yours

E. A. B.

84

BENNETT TO WELLS [*Printed announcement*]

With the compliments of Mr. & Mrs. Arnold Bennett
3 Rue D'Aumale, Paris

To announce the marriage of Mr. Arnold Bennett and Madame Marguerite Solié [*sic*], which took place the 4th of July, 1907, at the Mairie of the Ninth Arrondissement, Paris.

85

BENNETT TO MRS WELLS

37 *Clarendon Road*

5 *December* 1907   *Putney S.W.*

DEAR MRS. WELLS

Very many thanks for your most kind letter. We should very much like to come down between the 16th and the 21st, but unfortunately we can't; it is just between those dates that we are principally took up. Now if you could let us come down late in January or beginning of February we could do it. We are staying on in England because of my 5 Towns play which the Stage Society is producing.[1] I don't yet know exactly what we are going to do, but I know we shall be in England till the end of January at least.

L'Homme Invisible at 1 fr. is simply all *over* Paris like a rash. In fact it is all over France.

Perhaps you will let me hear from you in due course as to my suggestion.

Kindest regards to you both, and my wife's compliments (in French, that is).

Your sincerely
ARNOLD BENNETT

---

[1] *Cupid and Common-Sense*, a dramatisation of *Anna of the Five Towns*, produced by Frank Vernon for the Stage Society at the Shaftesbury Theatre, London, for two performances on 26 and 27 January 1908.

K

86

WELLS TO BENNETT

Spade House
Sandgate

[*December* 1907]

DEAR ARNOLD BENNETT

The book of *Things*[1] this year is better than ever.
A Very Happy New Year to you both and warmest good
wishes.

Yours ever
H. G.

Tell us when we are to see you.

87

BENNETT TO WELLS

3 *Ilchester Gardens*
[*London*]

2 *January* 1908

MY DEAR H. G.

It's like this. The play is to be produced at the
Shaftesbury Theatre Sunday evening 26th and Monday
matinee 27th. And we propose to return to France

[1] *Things Which Have Interested Me* [Second Series], which Ben-
nett had printed privately in Burslem and distributed to friends.
The first series was printed and issued in the same manner in
December 1906.

some day after that and to call on you on our way east-
wards—if it can be made convenient. When are you
both coming up?

You ought to see the play, as there is something in it.
The S. Society people make a fuss about giving me seats,
beyond the best box at each performance. I am going
to get some, but whether what I shall get will exceed the
demands of my family, I don't yet know. Can't you get
in "on your faces"? Surely you are running up to town
before then? If so, you both of you lunch or dine with
us.

Reciprocation of good honest wishes, et mes hommages à Madame.

Yours ever
E. A. B.

88

BENNETT TO MRS WELLS

14 *January* 1908   3 *Ilchester Gardens*

DEAR MRS. WELLS

Very many thanks. We should prefer to leave the date
for future settlement. Do I understand you will be up in
town about the 26, 27, 28? If so what day will you come
here to lunch or dinner? The play is produced on Sunday

26th and there is a matineé on the 27th. Have you got seats? Because if not, I must look after them.[1]

>Kindest regards
>Yours sincerely
>E. A. BENNETT

89

BENNETT TO MRS WELLS

Ilchester Mansions Hotel
1, 2 & 3 Ilchester Gardens
9 *February* 1908   *Bayswater, London, W.*
MY DEAR MRS. WELLS

Suppose we called on you on Tuesday March 3rd? That is the date on which we propose to quit this town. Will it do?

>Kindest regards to you both from us both.
>Yours sincerely
>ARNOLD BENNETT

[1] Wells saw the play. In a *Journal* entry of 1 February 1908 Bennett notes: "Wells was delighted, impressed rather deeply, I thought." (I, 277.)

90

BENNETT TO MRS WELLS

12 *February* 1908   3 *Ilchester Gardens W.*
MY DEAR MRS. WELLS

Many thanks. We shall be delighted to come on the
3rd and stay the night.

Our kindest regards to you both,
Yours sincerely,
ARNOLD BENNETT.

91

MRS BENNETT TO MRS WELLS

[Postscript from Bennett to Wells]
Les Sablons
6 *Mars* 1908   *près Moret*
Seine-et-Marne.

CHÈRE MADAME.

Merci pour l'hospitalité cordiale et charmante que vous
nous avez offerte. J'ai été heureuse de faire plus ample
connaissance avec vous et Mr G. H. [*sic*] Wells. Mon
mari assure que cette visite lui a fait beaucoup de bien. Je
peux très bien comprendre cela étant donné l'admiration
qu'il a pour votre mari.

Puisque j'ai eu l'avantage de faire le connaissance d'un des plus grands écrivains anglais en la personne de votre mari, je vais sous peu faire la connaissance de ses oeuvres dans leur langue originale. Notre voyage a été bon. La campagne est agréable malgré le mauvais temps.

Veuillez recevoir, chére Madame, mes sentiments les meilleurs.

MARGUERITE BENNETT

P.S. *New Worlds for Old*[1] is *simply magnificent*. It is certainly by far the best of its series, and it has moved me to an unusual enthusiasm. The only fault I have to find with it is that the word "extraordinarily" occurs in it 1,536,407 times.

The misprint specialist begs to point out that there is a howler on page 242—'procession' for 'precession'. Strange and lamentable that these lapses should happen! Receive the assurance of my affection for you all.

A. B.

92

WELLS TO BENNETT

Spade House

10 *July* [1908]   *Sandgate*

DEAR ARNOLD BENNETT

Buried Alive[2] is ripping good stuff. I have just been reading it. It's easy and skilful and humourous and daring

---

[1] 1908.   [2] 1908.

and everything it ought to be. You are having rather a boom in this house. The eminent Miss M. who has just come down from Cambridge covered with glories, Firsts in Part ii and so on, and who has hitherto been the devout admirer of *my* fiction has picked out *The Grim Smile of the Five Towns* and deserted. I am lending her *The Grand Babylon Hotel* and doing my best to hide the others.

Our warmest love to Madame.

H. G.

93

BENNETT TO WELLS [*Postcard*]

16 September 1908 [*Postmark*]

Gratified by your letter! I rely on you to cause *Premières et dernières choses* [1] to be sent to me. I will send you a truly *long* book [2] in return. We are *en voyage* in the Midi, after finishing the said book. Our greetings to you both.

BENNETT

---

[1] *First and Last Things, A Confession of Faith and Rule of Life*, 1908.

[2] *The Old Wives' Tale*. Bennett had begun the novel on 8 October 1907 at Les Sablons. He finished it at the Villa des Néfliers, Avon-Fontainebleau, on 30 August 1908.

94

WELLS TO BENNETT

Spade House

[*October* 1908]   *Sandgate*

First Notices

In the case of Important Books a larger Review will follow.

The Old Wives' Tale.[1] Ripping. Enormous various Balzac. Arnold has surpassed himself. No further question of *First Rank*. A great book and a big book. I will write further later. Nobody else could come anywhere near it. We are satisfied with our Bennett. There are only two real contemporary swell novelists under 50. He is one.

95

BENNETT TO WELLS

[*Villa des Néfliers*
Avon-Fontainebleau]

29 *October* 1908 [Postmark]   *Seine et Marne*

Well, the firm is duly grateful, and awaits details. It also awaits your book or books. It has a suspicion that they

[1] 1908.

or it have gone wrong owing to your notion of this address, which is

Villa des NÉFLIERS (medlar trees) not
　　„　„　Négliers.

Hueffer [1] has written to me about his *English Review*. Will his panoramic view of literature be sufficiently eagle-eyed to lead him to review *The O. Ws' Tale* in his reviews of a 'limited number' of books, think you?

We are writing a play about Harmsworth for the Stage Society.[2]

Love to all from us

E. A. B.

96

WELLS TO BENNETT

Spade House

[*November* 1908]   *Sandgate*

DEAR BENNETT.

I am going to write about *The O. W. T.* (which I repeat is a great book) later. This is to say that Hueffer says there is to be a review in the *second* number (the first is being printed) by a competent hand and that he agrees about the greatness.

Yours ever

H. G.

[1] Ford Madox Hueffer (later Ford), first editor of the *English Review*, in which Wells was very active. The first number appeared in December 1908.
[2] *What the Public Wants.*

97
WELLS TO BENNETT

Spade House

[*November* 1908]   *Sandgate*

MY DEAR BENNETT.

You know what life is. I have really wanted badly to write you at length about *The Old Wives' Tale* and make you understand that it isn't simply just genial mutual flattery and so forth that I want to send you this time. And days slip by and all sorts of things get in the way of that really satisfying old style letter. I think the book a quite pre-eminent novel so that it at least doubles your size in my estimation. It is far too big, too fine and too restrained to get at first anything like the recognition it is bound in the long run to bring you. It is the best book I have seen this year—and there have been one or two very good books—and I am certain it will secure you the respect of all the distinguished critics who are now consuming gripe-water and suchlike, if you never never write another line. It is all at such a high level that one does not know where to begin commending, but I think the high light for me is the bakehouse glimpse of Sam Povey.[1] But the knowledge, the detail, the spirit! from first to last it *never* fails.

[1] Book II, Chapter V.

I wish it could have gone into the *English Review*.
Well, I go round telling everyone I meet about it—I
wish Chapman & Hall would do the same. Go on great
man!

Yours ever
H. G.

98

BENNETT TO WELLS

Villa des Néfliers

Avon-Fontainebleau

18 *November* 1908

MY DEAR H. G.

What am I to say in reply to your remarks? Considerable emotion caused in this breast thereby! Also no
doubt a certain emotion in yours, as you cannot write
such letters often!

We must strive to live up to this. That is all.

Orage [1] has sent me your communication as to Frank
Harris. Naturally, I was the reviewer.[2] Harris was much
moved by the review, and came down here to see me. He
is certainly one of the most extraordinary men I ever met.

I am reading *1st and Last* which arrived a few days ago.
As it isn't a novel I can't pontificate on it. However,

---

[1] Alfred Richard Orage (1873–1934), editor of the *New Age*.
Bennett started "a column of book gossip" for the *New Age* on
18 March 1908. He wrote under the pen-name of Jacob Tonson.

[2] Harris's novel *The Bomb*, 1908.

when I have digested it I shall give you my ideas. There is no doubt whatever that it is a great deal too short, a very great deal. The *Westminster's* objections to its tone are merely silly. Its tone, like that of *New W. fr. Old*, is perfect.

Yours ever

E. A. B.

I am getting rather tired of the *Westminster*.

99

BENNETT TO WELLS

Villa des Néfliers

Avon S/M

23 *November* 1908

MY DEAR H. G.,

Those moments of "worship" (p. 50).[1] Of all the points in your book, this has most stuck in my mind. I wish you had enlarged on it, and not got out of it by referring to 'poverty of language.' I should like to have known what exactly you did mean—*do* mean. I regard this as the most important thing in the book, and it is not

[1] Bennett is referring to the following passage in *First and Last Things* (1908). "At times in the silence of the night and in rare lonely moments, I come upon a sort of communion of myself and something great that is not myself. It is perhaps poverty of mind and language obliges me to say that then this universal scheme takes on the effect of a sympathetic person—and my communion a quality of fearless worship. These moments happen, and they are the supreme fact in my religious life to me, they are the crown of my religious experiences."

really handled. I myself have never, at any rate for 25 years, had the slightest movement towards worship or anything resembling worship. This is why I want to know what people do feel in that line.

p. 85 and p. 90—Against immortality and transmigration of souls. I think you are too summary here. Having regard to the enormous philosophic ingenuity of Buddhistic and kindred dogma, I don't see how you can dismiss transmigration of souls as imaginings of "a race of children." [1] The memory difficulty has certainly been smoothed away for me. Here is another immensely important matter which I think you deal with too brusquely. By the way, I don't see the point of the references to Henley and Stevenson on p. 240. Personally (again) I am at present a believer in the transmigration of souls, as the theory which presents fewest difficulties. But if you can indicate to me any full attempt to make it seem impossible, I shall be glad to read the same.

After the above 2 matters, all others strike me as secondary.

There is an implied reference to 'Platonic' love on p. 211 which gives the reader to think that you think that Plato brought into prominence the notion of friendship between men and women. I do not think this is so. My idea is that the phrase 'platonic love' has been quite changed in mean-

[1] Bennett was to treat the subject of transmigration of souls, at least as it is expressed in Theosophy, extensively in *The Glimpse*, 1909.

ing, and that Plato meant something quite different and even more spiritual. In other words I think you have carried on a popular error. But I am not sure.

p. 169. "Plane of the barrack yard higher" etc. This is enormously ingenious and effective. But it does not convince me. In this military town I am a great watcher of soldiers, both in and out of barrack yards, and although what you say is all right so far as it goes, I would certainly put the plane of the barrack yard *much* lower than the plane outside. Your remarks on the future of war are A.1, and gave me light. The bit about cutting an atom in two with a knife is extraordinarily illuminating. This is what *I* call imagination.

Other matters that have stuck in my mind as being good, fine, helpful, are

43. The ethics of controversy. I remember you once sat on a Knight in the *Chronicle* for his crude notions of controversy.

79. The race walking in its sleep.

97. Gathering experience for the race.
    (But you don't say where it's stored, anti-transmigrationist)

148. Ingenuous reason for number of creeds in U.S.A.

192. Every theory has a finer offspring than itself.

245. *Thought has made me shameless.*

159. Against seceding.

195. All this against the popular notion of honour. You will wake many sympathies here, I bet.

156. No 'beginning afresh'.
196. Against 'justice' and litigiousness. I like this much.

As you are undoubtedly a litigious person by nature, this passage either speaks very well for your imaginative power, or it is simply an ingenuous index of the change going on in you. I think the latter. I think that *New W. for Old* and this book show an immense development, not in power, but in temper. They certainly increase one's *affection* for you.

It seems to me that you ought to make *1st and Last Things* a sort of annual, gradually enlarging it and keeping it up to date. It must be of real value to anybody not absolutely crystallised into a hard, definite form. But either it contains too much, or it is too short.

For me, you scarcely justify your inclusion of 'metaphysics.' Nor do I consider that your metaphysics really *are* metaphysics. Metaphysics are inseparably connected with ontological speculation, the perfection of whose futility is unmatched by the futility of anything else in the universe. Whereas your remarks deal with *phenomena*. No. I will acquit you of metaphysics.

I shall read it all again. I can only criticise *novels*. I wish I hadn't read the first part of *Tono-Bungay* [1] so *often*.

---

[1] Bennett must be referring to either the manuscript or proofs. *Tono-Bungay* was originally published in the *English Review* December 1908 to March 1909.

I shall have to read it yet again in order to get the hang of the last part.

We are going to Switzerland (Mont Pélerin, above Vevey) for Xmas. We come to Britain in March. I am just finishing a Stage Society Play, about the Yellow Press.[1]

Yours ever,

A. B.

100

WELLS TO BENNETT

[*December* 1908]

Spade House
Sandgate

DEAR BENNETT

Things [2] is very jolly, but not quite so intimate as the older model.

I have you very much on my conscience. I've a novel very much in hand and you know my gasteropodous [3] methods of writing. I've talked about *The Old Wives' Tale* to all sorts of people but I've not written a line anywhere. I'd have liked to. Everyone is reading it and everyone praises it except that old fool Colvin [4] who

[1] *What the Public Wants*, to be produced by the Stage Society on 2 May 1909, at the Aldwych Theatre, London.

[2] *Things Which Have Interested Me* [Third Series], printed privately at Burslem.

[3] The gasteropoda are a division of molluscs, including all snails and slugs.

[4] Sidney Colvin (1845–1927), Keeper of Prints and Drawings, British Museum, biographer of Keats, and editor of Robert Louis Stevenson's correspondence.

detects French models and says its dreadfully heartless (not like dear R. L. S.). That fool Hueffer[1] too isn't doing a shout about it in the *English Review*. I did all I could (short of writing it myself) to get the book done for number 2, but he's got a discovery of his own, a man named Reynolds[2] of about Edwin Pugh's calibre and apparently he's giving up the Famed *Review* to him.

Well, God give you a Happy New Year and Madame also.

Yours ever

H. G.

IOI

BENNETT TO WELLS

Grand Hôtel Belvédère

Mont-Pélerin-sur-Vevey

7 *January* 1909

MY DEAR H. G.

Many thanks. Someone has been doing some spade-work for *The Old Wives' Tale*, so I put it down to you. I expected it to be an absolute frost, naturally, and it was at first. But after about a month it began to sell. It went into a modest second edition, and the last I hear is that it is still selling regularly. Anyhow, I have had some

---

[1] Wells and Hueffer were at this time in serious disagreement over the financing, editing, and publication of *Tono-Bungay* in the *English Review*.

[2] Stephen Reynolds (1881–1919), author of *A Poor Man's House*, 1908, a novel about Devon fishermen and other books.

really pleasing reviews. Of course any article from you would have been butter on my bread. I think enough has been said about Stephen Reynolds for some time to come. But I put him very much higher than Edwin Pugh, and I have a great admiration for him. I don't know yet about Hueffer, but I'm sure the *English Review* won't last unless he alters it considerably. I've written him an A1 short story,[1] which he had the wit to commission, so that I will partly forgive him for not trumpeting the book. I am informed that my new play is 'simply terrific.'[2] Why can't you come over to Switzerland *now*, and have a time?

Our loves to you both
Yours ever,
E. A. B.

[1] "The Matador of the Five Towns," *English Review*, April 1909.
[2] *What the Public Wants.*

102

WELLS TO BENNETT

Spade House
[*Early April* 1909]   *Sandgate*

DEAR BENNETT

    Come and have lunch at the *Reform Club* (Pall Mall)
at 1.45 on Friday.

Ever thine
H. G.

103

BENNETT TO MRS WELLS

37 Clarendon Road
4 *April* 1909   *Putney S.W.*

DEAR MRS. WELLS

    H. G. and I arranged, subject to your ideas on the
subject, that Marguerite and I should come down to you
on the 21st (with two toothbrushes) for the night. He
told me to enter into negotiations with you on the subject. And I hereby do.

        Our kindest regards and best wishes.

Yours sincerely
ARNOLD BENNETT

104

WELLS TO BENNETT [*Postcard*]

6 *April* 1909
Spade House
Sandgate

DEAR BENNETT

The Reform Club committee (because of Easter) does not meet until the 22nd, after which you'll be a Reform 'Clubber.' [1] But that will give you a club after the N.L.C. [2] has expired.

Yours ever

H. G.

Your seconder is H. Arthur Jones. [3]

Warmest regards to Madame.

[1] After his lunch with Wells on Friday, 4 April, Bennett noted in his *Journal*, "I wanted to belong to this club." But Wells's attempt was, in this instance, unsuccessful. See letter No. 126, October 1912.

[2] National Liberal Club.

[3] Henry Arthur Jones (1851–1929), successful playwright of the time.

105

BENNETT TO WELLS

Villa des Néfliers

11 *June* 1909   *Avon S/M*

MY DEAR H. G.

Now I was just going to write and tell you how *The W. in the Air* [1] had held and impressed me, when I got your post card. And couldn't. Still, I was very glad to have the p.c. I shall not be content if you do not see *What the Public Wants*, even in Hawtrey's [2] absurd interpretation of it. If you demand seats, in my name, of "Lyston Lyle Esq," at the Royalty Theatre, he is instructed to supply you. Go soon, as I cannot conceive that it will run long. You will be able to read the play entire in the *English Review* of July—I am told. [3]

Loves from us both to you both.

Yours

A. B.

[1] *The War in the Air*, 1908.
[2] Charles Hawtrey, actor and manager. He played James Hearn's original part, Sir Charles Morgan, in the Royalty Theatre production of the play.
[3] *What the Public Wants* did appear as a supplement to the July number of the *English Review*.

106

WELLS TO BENNETT

[*July* 1909]   *National Liberal Club*

DEAR OLD BENNETT.

I don't like the growing tendency in my letters to break into praise. It is unseemly between great men. I feel I don't see enough of you and hence these veracities in the place of the old familiar abuse. I took Jane to your play last night and cuddled myself with pleasure most of the time. Its effect is of being studded with good things. Someone (Wm Archer I think) said it was damaged by Hawtrey but I don't think so nor does Jane—which is better seeing she saw the Sunday night performance. He's a "real creation". But your lines are so damned good —I who know you am astonished. You are the least appreciated man in London. I advise any intelligent investor to buy Bennetts for a rise. The only serious objection I have to the play (Archer J. agreeing) is that they don't make such men in the Five Towns, and that the home ought to have been in Kilburn. It seems to me you are just a little timid in going to the Five Towns always for your homes and domesticities. I throw out the hint.

Bennett—Wells—who else is there? A young poet named Steevens [1] is said to have arisen in Dublin. We are the last of an age otherwise. And by the bye, it may interest you to know that that affair of philoprogenitive passion isn't over. (You will remember the affair.) Interesting and remarkable psychological reactions followed. The two principals appear to have underestimated the web of affections and memories that held them together. The husband, a perfectly admirable man, being married attempted to play a husband's part— (which was asinine of him). Violent emotional storms have ensued and there is a separation and I think it will be necessary out of common fairness to him to give him grounds and have a divorce—and run a country cottage in the sight of all mankind. I tell you these things to strain your continence, knowing you will tell no one and suffer dreadful things not doing so. I have sold Spade House and got a delightful house in Church Row Hampstead for Jane. We shall go there in August I expect. I am extremely happy and I have never worked so well.

Yours ever

H. G.

[1] James Stephens, whose *Insurrections*, a book of verse, was published in 1909.

107

WELLS TO BENNETT

17 *Church Row*

[20 *October* 1909]   *Hampstead* [1]

DEAR BENNETT.

I can't quite begin *The Glimpse* [2] yet. I am urged to in the enclosed.[3] The Taggy referred to is Ellis MacTaggart a benighted Hegelian at Cambridge [4] and the letter goes on to refer to our child as a different sort of basis altogether. I've dipped into the chapter called "A Drama" and it doesn't strike me as beautiful a bit—beastly words like vermilion—nasty opaque salt of mercury. But since I respect both you and M. profoundly I'll do as she says and go through it. Are you coming to London soon? I want to see you. Beautiful prismatic *situations* develop and dissolve round me and M. and the coarse fact remains that everything is going very well.

Yours ever

H. G.

[1] Wells had sold Spade House in May. The family moved into 17 Church Row, Hampstead, in August 1909.

[2] Bennett's *The Glimpse, an Adventure of the Soul*, 1909. In his autobiography Wells describes the book as "a glimpse into an empty cavern in his mind." (II, 628–629.)

[3] Presumably a letter to Wells from M.

[4] John M'Taggart Ellis M'Taggart (1866–1925), Fellow of the British Academy and of Trinity College, Cambridge.

108

WELLS TO BENNETT

17 *Church Row*
5 *January* 1910   *Hampstead*

DEAR BENNETT.

God keeps me busy in London just now. Good luck
to you at Brighton and let us know directly you have
dates for London again. Perhaps Madam will come to
dinner on the way back. We'd greatly like to see her.

Yours ever

H. G. WELLS

109

BENNETT TO WELLS

13 *March* 1910   *Royal York Hotel*
Ansᵈ. but to write V.L.   *Brighton*
[*Wells's note*]

MY DEAR H. G.

Does Vernon Lee [1] live in Florence? Does she know
anything about me? Would she be a useful person to
know there? If yes, perhaps you wouldn't mind sending

[1] Pseudonym of Violet Paget (1856–1935), English author and
art critic, who lived in Italy for most of her life. She had been a
guest in Wells's home and had written "On Modern Utopias, an
Open Letter to H. G. Wells," in the *Fortnightly Review*, December
1906, a commentary on Wells's *A Modern Utopia*.

me a letter of credit to her. We leave here on Friday and shall get to Florence at the end of the month. We're sorry we haven't seen you. I only went up to London to see a Fancy Dress Ball and came back the next afternoon. I've written 100,000 words here in 10 weeks. I expect we shall be over in London again in the autumn, as after long ineffectual efforts to get me to alter the play I wrote for them,[1] the Haymarket people have decided to produce it as it is.

Affection to you both

Yours

A. B.

My new book [2] is not important enough to send you without a special request.

IIO

WELLS TO BENNETT

17 Church Row

[*Received* 4 *October* 1910]   *Hampstead*

DEAR BENNETT

Why no *Clayhanger*? [3] What have I done? Here is everyone talking of *Clayhanger* and me silent.

[1] *The Honeymoon*, a comedy in three acts. The Haymarket Theatre later sold the play, without producing it, to J. E. Vedrenne and Dennis Eadie, who produced it at the Royalty Theatre, 6 October 1911.

[2] *Helen with the High Hand, an Idyllic Diversion*, 1910.

[3] September 1910.

Which reminds me that old Radford, (Father of various daughters you met here) Ernest Radford[1] wants to seek you out and see you. His address is Hotel d'Orleans, Rue Jacob, Paris.

Can you give him an appointment.

Yours ever

H. G. WELLS

III

BENNETT TO WELLS

Villa des Néfliers

4 *October* 1910   *Avon-Fontainebleau*

MY DEAR H. G.

Nothing but a slightly different arrangement this time. My immediate relatives copped my English copies, save 2, which I keep, and I ordered that American copies should be sent to you and a few other select recipients. Then the American publication got itself delayed. Hence these tears. However, I understand the American edition is now out, and you will have your 699 pages in a few days. By the way, whatever people may say, and whatever this edition may look like, you may take it authoritatively

---

[1] A lecturer on English architecture and one-time secretary of the Arts and Crafts Exhibition Society. He was also a minor poet, a member of the Fabian Society, and, from contemporary accounts, very much an eccentric. Bennett had met Mrs. Radford and her daughters when dining with the Wellses on 21 December 1909.

from me that this book is only 160,000 words long, 40,000 words shorter than *The O.W. Tale*.

I write to Ernest *père* and ask him to lunch.

Our love to you both

Yours

A. B.

P.S. When is *The New M*[1] going to appear? I shall take care, this time, that the *New Age* does not make a fool of itself.

112

WELLS TO BENNETT

17 *Church Row*

[*December* 1910]   *Hampstead*
DEAR BENNETT.

The Few Great Minds in the world should react upon each other more. I'm going with the whole blessed family to Davos for January to luge and suchlike. Why not spend your January in Davos or Klosters also?

Yours ever,

H. G.

I have tons to say about *Clayhanger* for example.

[1] *The New Machiavelli*, January 1911.

113

BENNETT TO WELLS

59 Rue de Grenelle [1]

17 *January* 1911   *Paris*

MY DEAR H. G.

I got *The New M* the day before yesterday, and have read the first book and am enthusiastic thereupon. But this is not what I am writing about. I am asked to do an anti-censorship, anti-puritan article for the *English Review*.[2] Is there anything that you specially think ought to be said, or that you want saying? For instance about you.

Frightfully busy on *Hilda Lessways*,[3] if you remember her.

Loves to all

Yours

A BENNETT

[1] The Bennetts moved into a furnished flat at this address in November 1910.

[2] The article, if Bennett wrote it, never appeared in the *English Review*.

[3] The sequel to *Clayhanger*, 1911.

114

BENNETT TO MRS WELLS

Authors' Club
2 Whitehall Court,
19 *April* 1911   *SW*
DEAR MRS. WELLS

This is disastrous. I have been about and about without an address and have only just got yours of the 6th. I
left Paris on the 7th. I can't write to Mrs. Lane as I have
no feasible address for her, but perhaps you will give me
one, so that I can apologise. My wife is coming here next
week, and we expect to stay until June 15th. I have come
here because through this Club one can get rooms rather
nicely in "the finest situation in London." A strange
place! Charles Garvice,[1] patting me on the back, has just
said to me: "The secret of your success, my boy, as of
every success since Shakespere, is your universal sympathy." He then told me 6,000,000 copies of his own
works had been sold, but he is very modest about them.
If you are in one night after dinner I will come up. You
can telephone any message: if I am not in, the august
head-waiter, one Dali, will take it.

                              Loves to all
                              Yours always
                              ARNOLD BENNETT
[1] Prolific English journalist, novelist, and playwright (1883–1920).

115

MRS BENNETT TO MRS WELLS

11 *May* 1911   2 *Whitehall Court, S.W.*
CHÈRE MADAME:

Vous nous ferez grand plaisir en venant dîner avec nous Vendredi prochain 19 Mai, à 7.30.

Nous aurons Mr. Turner [1] et Mrs. Belloc-Lowndes.[2]

Nous nous réunirons dans le salon de l'immeuble.

Bien sincèrement à vous

MARGUERITE BENNETT

116

BENNETT TO MRS WELLS

Villa des Néfliers
29 *June* 1911   *Avon S/M*
MY DEAR MRS. WELLS

It was impossible for me to call en route. Can I come one day next week, Tuesday, Wednesday, Thursday or Friday, for the night (without ceremonious clothes)? I

---

[1] Probably Reginald Turner (1872–1938) friend of Oscar Wilde and Max Beerbohm.

[2] The novelist (1868–1947). Her best-known novels are *The Chink in the Armour* (1912) and *The Lodger* (1913). She was the sister of Hilaire Belloc.

have to go to Paris. There is a train from Paris which gets to Pont de l'Arche [1] a little before 7. If you are far from the station perhaps a carriage could be sent to meet me. I should leave the next day at 4 p.m. Very busy.

With kindest regards to all

Yours sincerely

ARNOLD BENNETT

117

BENNETT TO MRS WELLS

Villa des Néfliers

Saturday 3 *July* 1911 [Postmark]   *Avon S/M*

DEAR MRS. WELLS

Many thanks. I shall come *Tuesday*, by the train that arrives a little before 7. I can't come by the earlier train as I have to lunch in Paris.

Kindest regards

Yours sincerely

ARNOLD BENNETT

LATER Having regard to the Railway disorganization down your way, I will come THURSDAY instead of Tuesday.

AB

[1] The Wellses stayed there from June to October 1911.

118

BENNETT TO MRS WELLS

Villa des Néfliers

Avon

Mardi soir 5 *July* 1911 [Postmark]   *S et M.*

CHÈRE MADAME

Donc, j'arriverai jeudi soir par le train de 6.54. Si c'est possible de prendre un train plus tôt, je vous telegrapherai.

Toujour votre devoué

ARNOLD BENNETT

119

BENNETT TO MRS WELLS

Villa des Néfliers

Saturday [8 *July* 1911]   *Avon-Fontainebleau*

DEAR MRS. WELLS,

My train ran off the line at Mantes.[1] First two coaches pitched over. Front part of my coach telescoped, and the whole coach smashed. For a few seconds I was in a storm of glass, flying doors, and hand-luggage. All over in ten seconds. A woman in front part of my coach had her leg broken. Having seen what there was to see, I hired an

[1] Nearly twenty years later Bennett used this incident as the basis of his novel *Accident*, 1928.

M

auto for 100 *frs*, and sold 3 places in it for 70 *fr*. and thus got to Paris for 30 *frs*. only a quarter of an hour late for dinner! Still I don't want to be in any more railway accidents. The only account that I have seen of the accident, in the *Figaro*, is inaccurate in every detail except the number of wounded.

I don't travel again on the Ouest-Etat for some years to come.

You will let us know which day you are coming here.

Kind regards to your mother and to Mrs. Bowkett.

Love from us to the rest

Yours sincerely

ARNOLD BENNETT

120

BENNETT TO MRS WELLS

Grand Hotel Californie [1]

17 *February* 1912   *Cannes*

DEAR MRS. WELLS,

Many thanks for your letter.

Inflammation of the intestines.

Convalescent.

Strict regime.

---

[1] Bennett had returned from a successful six-weeks tour of America in November 1911. He went to Cannes to await the completion of his house at Thorpe-le-Soken. The illness he speaks of was later thought to have been undiagnosed typhoid.

But working.

Just began the further adventures of Edward Henry Machin,[1] but my joy therein is clouded by the news that influenza has reduced you to shadows. Kindly become substantial once more.

I shall be charmed to have the proofs, and to know about how long I can keep them. Phillips [2] of the *American Mag*, a most delightful man, stated with sad resignation to me that he had not been able to get any corrected proofs out of H.G.[3] Or such is my recollection. However, I told him how great H.G. was, and he seemed comforted.

Nos sympathies le plus chaudes,

ARNOLD BENNETT

121

BENNETT TO MRS WELLS

Hotel Californie

20 *March* 1912   *Cannes*

DEAR MRS. WELLS,

I return the proofs [4] by registered bookpost. I have read them with care. I have of course confined my ob-

---

[1] Hero of *The Card*, 1911, and its sequel, *The Regent*, 1913, which Bennett speaks of here.

[2] John S. Phillips, an editor of the *American Magazine*.

[3] For *Marriage*, 1912.

[4] In a letter to a friend, 14 March 1912, Bennett had written: "By the way, Wells's new novel, *Marriage*, of which I have just read the

servations to misprints, punctuation, points of phrase-ology, and sentences of which I absolutely failed to grasp the meaning. I daresay H. G. may consider some of my criticisms as a proof-reader beneath notice, but having regard to his great onslaught, in the novel, on the general sloppiness of everything except pure research, I think it may be worth his while to consider them. I have had to disfigure the proofs with my remarks, as a mere question note would not have made my suggestion clear always. You can rub them out if the worst comes to the worst, as they are all in pencil.

I had great difficulty in correcting some parts as I was too interested in the narrative to fix my mind on H.G.'s shortcomings as a writer who knows the details of his business. The Labrador episode ought by all the theory of chances to have been a failure, but I don't think it is. It held me throughout. But then I am an *admirer* of H. G.— probably the best he has. Anyhow I am a thundering good proof reader!

Yours sincerely,

ARNOLD BENNETT

P.S. Where I have put in punctuation without a query, I think the question is beyond argument.

---

proofs, contains more intimate conveyances of the *atmosphere* of married life than anybody has ever achieved before. I am rather annoyed as I am about to get the same intimacy in my Clayhanger–Hilda book entitled *These Twain*. These coincidences are distressing." (Pound, p. 238.)

122

BENNETT TO WELLS

Hotel Californie

21 *March* 1912   *Cannes*

DEAR FATHER,

No, they[1] have not got me at all. Under no circum-
stances would I countenance this grotesque Institution.
I suppose you never read my deathless article on it in the
New Age 19 months ago. Go ahead and make a row.

Yours

E. A. B.

[1] The Academic Committee of the Royal Society of Literature
of the United Kingdom. Wells had received a letter from Edmund
Gosse on 18 March stating: "I have the great pleasure of telling you
that you have been elected a member of the Academic Committee,
a matter on which Henry James and I have long set our hearts."
Wells had written in the 28 September 1911 issue of the *Eye-Witness*
a satirical article on the Academic Committee, pointing out its
insignificance in relation to the "broad flow of able writing and
creative work that is now going on," but seeing some remote
danger of its forming a core for a committee on the censorship of
books.

123

WELLS TO BENNETT

17 Church Row

Hampstead

[25 *March* 1912]

MY DEAR BENNETT.

Your corrections are wonderful and precious. You have the best mind in Europe (in many respects) and I thank you very gratefully. And here is a letter [1] (which please return) which will explain why, although I inflexibly won't be elected to that absurd body, I am not making a violent assault upon it for its impudence.

Yours ever fraternally

H. G. WELLS

124

BENNETT TO WELLS

Hotel Californie

Cannes

27 *March* 1912

MY DEAR H. G.,

Many thanks. I return the letter. C'est touchant. Mind they aren't too many for you, yet!

We shall arrive in England on Apl 30th.

Thine

A. B.

[1] Wells enclosed a letter from Henry James, dated 20 March, urging him to reconsider his refusal to accept membership of the

125

WELLS TO BENNETT

Little Easton Rectory

[*September* 1912]   *Dunmow* [1]

DEAR BENNETT

Glad indeed you are going to be almost neighbours.[2]
We're rooting here firmly. Can you lunch with me at the
Reform Club on Wednesday, Thursday or Friday in
next week? If so, I'll get James [3] to come. He wants
badly to meet you.

Yours ever

H. G.

Royal Society of Literature. For the correspondence between
Wells and James on this matter, see *Henry James and H. G. Wells*,
edited by Leon Edel and Gordon N. Ray, 1958, pp. 157–164.

[1] In Essex Wells had first acquired Little Easton Rectory as an
occasional retreat from London, but soon removed his family there,
changing the name to Easton Glebe. It remained Wells's permanent
home until 1930.

[2] Bennett was to move into Comarques, Thorpe-le-Soken, on
25 February 1913. Comarques was an early Queen Anne house on
the Essex coast. At this time it was being remodelled by Bennett's
friend E. A. Rickards.

[3] Henry James. But James was ill, and was not to meet Bennett
until more than two months later. See *Henry James and H. G.
Wells*, p. 165.

126

WELLS TO BENNETT

Little Easton Rectory

[*October* 1912]   *Dunmow*

MY DEAR BENNETT.

James herewith.[1] Let's make it then a foursome and bring our wives. Will you? *Royal Automobile* Friday 1.30.

About the *Reform* you will not get elected if I propose you. But I will speak to one or two more generally popular persons in the matter.

Yours ever

H. G. WELLS

[1] Wells no doubt enclosed the letter from Henry James, dated 18 October 1912, expressing James's regret at not being able to attend the luncheon referred to in letter 125 and also expressing a desire to meet Bennett in the near future. See *Henry James and H. G. Wells*, pp. 165–166.

127

BENNETT TO WELLS

16 *December* 1912   14 *St Simon's Avenue*
                                        Putney S.W.
MY DEAR H.G.,

I return the proofs.[1] As before, all suggestions are
tentative. But when I have made a definite correction
without querying it, I have assumed that you could not
possibly contest its propriety. You may go on your way
rejoicing about this book. It is all right, especially the
difficult parts. I should judge it to be rather better than
Marriage—certainly more homogeneous—and about as
good as *The New M*; only it contains nothing so uncon-
vincing as the hero's change of party in *The New M*. I
think there are one or two short weak passages—such as
the page or two in Paris, and a few pages towards the end,
but naught to speak of. Mary is immense—and so are
her letters. What is fine about the darned thing, and what
is fine after your previous 2 or 3 darned things, is the
generosity and reasonableness of its spirit,—especially the
generosity. I have never seen this certainly outstanding
quality praised in any review. Yet there it is plain enough.

We go to Paris in a few days for 10 days. We expect to
be at Thorpe-le-Soken about Feb 15th. Let's know if
you will be in London during January.   Yours

                                                A. B.

[1] Of *The Passionate Friends*, 1913.

128

WELLS TO BENNETT

[*December* 1912]   *Little Easton Rectory*
                                             Dunmow
MY DEAR A. B.

Many thanks. Your precisions are wonderful and nearly all I have accepted with eager gratitude. But Peninsular War is right. I'm glad you like the book, which I mistrust myself as the end of a phase. The next will be quite different and longer. We are Christmasing here and going to Switzerland until early February.

                                        Yours ever
                                             H. G.

129

BENNETT TO MRS WELLS

13 *November* 1913   *Comarques*
                                      Thorpe-le-Soken
DEAR MRS. WELLS

Are you in town on Wednesday afternoon, 19th? If so, I should like to send you tickets for a *really* good chamber concert [1] at Bechstein Hall. In haste.

                                      Yours sincerely,
                                        ARNOLD BENNETT

[1] By Cedric Sharpe, the well-known cellist, and an old friend of Bennett.

130

BENNETT TO WELLS [*Postcard*]

7 *April* 1914

Yacht Velsa
Portoferraio

SIR,

I am deeply touched by this mark of your regard. I have heard from your young friend, and have written to him duly.

Elba is a divine spot, in a ditto climate.

Thine

A. B.

131

BENNETT TO MRS WELLS

15 *July* 1915

Comarques
Thorpe-le-Soken

DEAR MRS. WELLS

So sorry. I have been away at the Front for over three weeks without an address. If it isn't too late I shall be very glad indeed to read through the proofs.[1] So please send them to me.

We are in extreme health and hope you are.

Great haste

Yours sincerely

ARNOLD BENNETT

[1] Of *The Research Magnificent*, 1915.

132

BENNETT TO MRS WELLS

Comarques

25 *July* 1915   *Thorpe-le-Soken*

DEAR MRS. WELLS,

I sent yesterday the first 240 pages and I hope that they have reached you safely. I expect to be able to send the remainder in about a week. Of course it is clearly understood that, with the exception of the correction of a few obvious misprints, all my alterations are simply in the nature of respectful suggestions. I do not expect to be out of bed until Tuesday. I have had another attack of inflammation of the colon, as a result of my visit to the French and English lines.

Yours sincerely

ARNOLD BENNETT

133

BENNETT TO MRS WELLS

Comarques

1 *August* 1915   *Thorpe-le-Soken*

DEAR MRS. WELLS,

I enclose the remainder of the proofs. This novel is consistently and thoroughly interesting. I am just crawling about again. My work is gravely in arrears. I hope to write you soon about coming over. The difficulty is that our chauffeur is now an armed man, and we have to shove ourselves. We have put the big car in store, and are contenting ourselves with a Ford.

Yours sincerely,
ARNOLD BENNETT

134

BENNETT TO WELLS

Comarques
Thorpe-le-Soken

4 *October* 1915

MY DEAR H. G.

Marguerite can't come as she has arranged to go to London on Saturday. But I can, especially as I shall be alone and will therefore drive over on Saturday morning (I think—if I change to the afternoon I'll let you know). I like your remark about the Reform Club. The R. C. has been closed for a month and only reopened last Friday, so that your attempt to persuade me that you have been practically living there during September fails. Up to September I regularly attended the said Club on Fridays. Many thanks for the inscribed *R.M.*[1] Have I

---

[1] *The Research Magnificent.*

told you this is a good book? I send you a bookling just out.[1]

Our respex to Madam

Thine

A. B.

P.S. We have been on the eve of coming over for about 6 weeks. But the day never dawned.

A. B.

135

BENNETT TO MRS WELLS

Comarques

11 *October* 1915   *Thorpe-le-Soken*

MY DEAR LADY

I leapt on the *Sunday Times*. All the indiscretions were in it, including the worst, so I suppose all is now over between you and H.G.[2] I suggest that you both come here to make it up again. I have described fully to Marguerite my weekend, and she now regrets that she did not unscrupulously chuck London and come with me. She also wants to know when I have arranged for you two to come over here. When *have* I arranged that for? It has to occur, you know, hateful as the prospect must

---

[1] Probably *The Author's Craft*, October 1915.

[2] A careful perusal of the *Sunday Times* of 10 October 1915 yielded no explanation for this allusion.

be to you. *I desire a straight answer to this.*[1] Any week-end or any week-middle will suit us. You will not enjoy yourselves as much as I did, but you will have to go through with it.

Yours ever

A. B.

I arrived at 11.40, and wrote my article this afternoon.

136

BENNETT TO MRS WELLS

Comarques

3 *December* 1915   *Thorpe-le-Soken*

DEAR MRS. WELLS,

I wish I could.[2] But I am going to Manchester on Monday and have to write my *D.N.*[3] article on Sunday. Give my love to Frank please.

Ever yours

ARNOLD BENNETT

[1] Mrs Wells interjects a note: "Can you reply to him?" At the top of the page Wells writes "Monday week i.e. 25th."

[2] In reply to an invitation to spend the weekend at Easton. The "Frank" referred to at the end of the note is Frank Richard Wells.

[3] *Daily News.*

137

BENNETT TO MRS WELLS

Comarques

29 *January* 1916   *Thorpe-le-Soken*

DEAR MRS. WELLS

If you should feel inclined to help in the enclosed concert,[1] I should be very much obliged, as I am organising it. It is the first concert I have ever handled, and, though it promises excellently, it will be the last.

I fear hockey is off for the present.[2] I am too busy.

Our affections

A. B.

[1] At the Haymarket Theatre for the Wounded Allies Relief Committee on 21 February. He noted in his *Journal*, "This went off without a hitch, and I was very glad when it was over. I had no particular trouble but I will never organise another." (II, 154.) He was on the Executive Committee of the group, to which he devoted a great deal of time, attending meetings and assisting with the arrangements of a number of fund-raising events, including selling books on a stall at a War Fair held at the Caledonian Market on a rainy morning.

[2] The week-end hockey at Easton Glebe was an institution, enjoyed by friends, and, during the war, by members of the armed forces stationed nearby. Frank Swinnerton wrote of Easton weekends, "In winter whole hockey teams would come in chars-a-banc, until the lawns were black as with the expulsion of trippers from an excursion train." *An Autobiography* (1936), p. 159.

138

BENNETT TO MRS WELLS

Comarques
26 *June* 1916   *Thorpe-le-Soken*

DEAR MRS. WELLS,

It shall be done.[1] H. G. told me there was no breath-
less hurry.

Yours sincerely,
ARNOLD BENNETT

139

BENNETT TO WELLS

Comarques
[*June* 1916]   *Thorpe-le-Soken*

This book is all right.

A. B.

P.S. Unless it goes to pieces at the end. More to follow.

[1] The proofs of *Mr. Britling Sees It Through.*

N

140

BENNETT TO WELLS

6 July 1916   *Thorpe-le-Soken*

DEAR HERBERT,

Will you be at the Club next Thursday, 13th? If so will you lunch with me and Seebohm Rowntree, superintendent of the "Welfare" Department of Ministry of Munitions?

I shall finish your proofs on Saturday.

Thine

A. B.

141

BENNETT TO WELLS

Comarques

8 July 1916   *Thorpe-le-Soken*

MY DEAR HERBERT,

I like this book very much.[1] It is extremely original and sympathetic, and the scenes that ought to be the best are the best. In fact it is an impressive work. (I doubt if Direck [2] is anything like upon the level of the other

---

[1] *Mr. Britling See It Through*, 1916.
[2] An American visitor at Britling's.

characters as a creation.) Also as a tract it is jolly fine. It would have been even finer if old Brit had made the slightest attempt imaginatively to understand the difficulties of the British Government, or what it *did* do. If he had given to this business a quarter of the skill and force which he gives to understanding what it failed to do, he would have been liker God. Also his notions about the "steely resolution" of the French nation are a bit *Morning-Postish*. I say this because I know it would anger him. There is much more steely resolution in England than in France. The spirit of Paris has not been good. The spirit of the Midi has been rotten. This I know of my own knowledge. What has saved France is nothing but the accident of first-rate generalship. If the Battle of the Marne had been lost there wouldn't have been even a semblance of steely resolution in France. Even after the Marne every military set-back has been instantly followed by a civil crisis. Much more might be said on these two points, but old Brit shall not be harried.

Thine

A. B.

P.S. You will doubtless find some of the corrections quite inadmissible.

They are all simply suggestions.

AB

142

WELLS TO BENNETT

[*November* 1916] 16a *John Street*

DEAR ARNOLD

Mrs Haden Guest to whom I am giving this letter is one of those noosances who get up books for France and things. She is late in the field with the nicest of all, a book about Belgium, and I have done her some lively pictures, of which she will enclose proofs. Her book is called the *Princess Marie Jose's Children's Book*.[1] She wants you to write a short beautiful letter to the press on behalf of her book, which she can have typed and sent out to the press. She is a great dear and I like her very much.

Please do so

Your affectionate Uncle

H. G.

[1] *Princess Marie José's Children's Book* (for the Vestiaire Marie José, a Society for providing Milk, Food and Clothes to the Babies behind the firing line in Flanders), November 1916. The book contains a short story by Wells, "Master Anthony and the Zeppelin," illustrated by the author.

143

BENNETT TO WELLS [*Postcard*]

21 *November* 1916   *Thorpe-le-Soken*

Marguerite has ventured to give your name as a reference to flat-landlords. Thanks.

ARNOLD BENNETT

144

BENNETT TO MRS WELLS

24 *May* 1917   *Thorpe-le-Soken*

DEAR MRS. WELLS,

Will you come and have lunch with J. C. Squire, Elizabeth Asquith and me at il Ristorante del Commercio, 63 Frith St. Soho, on *Wednesday* next at 1.30, upstairs? I shall be very pleased if you will.

Yours sincerely
ARNOLD BENNETT

145

BENNETT TO WELLS

Ministry of Information
Norfolk Street
15 *July* 1918   *Strand.*

MY DEAR H. G.,

A further article by me on the League of Nations will appear in the *Daily News* tomorrow (Tuesday). I hope it will suit you.

Let me remind you that you are dining with me at the Royal Thames Yacht Club, 60 Picadilly, on Wednesday night at 8 o'clock.

Thine

A. B.

146

WELLS TO BENNETT

Crewe House
16 *July* 1918   *Curzon Street, W.*1.

DEAR ARNOLD,

The article is excellent.

Yours very sincerely,
H. G. WELLS

147

WELLS TO BENNETT

[*Typewritten circular, with salutation written in longhand*]
LEAGUE OF FREE NATIONS ASSOCIATION

22 *Buckingham Gate*
[25 *July* 1918]   *S.W.*1.

DEAR ARNOLD

I am sending you a manifesto of the Aims and Objects of the League of Free Nations Association, and I sincerely hope that you will be able to see your way to become an original member of the Council which is to be the governing body of the Association.

As you know there are so many definitions of what a League of Nations is supposed to be and what it is supposed to do, that we have endeavoured to set forth a basis upon which the structure can be built, and to focus all shades of public opinion on this vital question. We are also anxious to co-operate with kindred movements in allied and neutral countries, in order that pressure may be brought upon the respective governments to come into line before the war is at an end.

May I express the hope that you will be able to collaborate with us?

There is no intention on our part to compete with the League of Nations Society, or any other Society or Organization whose principles embody the ideal we are aiming at, which exists for the definite objects set forth in the basis of their Constitution. We hope to co-operate with them, and there does not appear to be any reason why both Societies should not act side by side in this matter, and give each other all the mutual help they possibly can.

Yours ever

H. G.

148

BENNETT TO WELLS

27 *July* 1918

MY DEAR H. G.

I reply to your circular. I will gladly join the League of Free Nations Association. It will, however, be impossible for me to attend the meetings, as I am already grossly overworked. I am sending a formal application for membership, with a subscription, directly to the Association.

Yours
A. B.

149

WELLS TO BENNETT

Easton Glebe,
Dunmow

[28 *July* 1918]

DEAR ARNOLD

You do not grasp the honour done you. You have been invited to join the Council of the L. of F. N. Assn. Please do.

Yours ever
H. G.

150

WELLS TO BENNETT

Easton Glebe,
Dunmow

[*September* 1918]

DEAR ARNOLD

Yes. Let's warm Beans his ear.[1] Frank knows no Russian. 2 hours a week is preposterous.

Yours ever

H. G.

I'm writing to Beans. Strongly.

---

[1] F. W. Sanderson, Headmaster of Oundle School, "who was always known to his scholars as 'Beans,' but H. G. Wells and A. B. called him The Marquis of Beans." (Richard Bennett in *Arnold Bennett's Letters to His Nephew*, 1936.) Richard Bennett and Wells's sons were attending Oundle at this time. On 9 September 1918 Sanderson replied to a letter from Wells in which Wells urged strongly that Gyp be given at least six hours of Russian a week. Wells, who was extremely interested in Sanderson's new methods and ideas in education, published a biography, *The Story of a Great Schoolmaster* (1924), shortly after Sanderson's sudden death. Sanderson is also the prototype of Job Huss in *The Undying Fire*, 1919.

151

BENNETT TO WELLS

22 *February* 1919   17 *Berkeley W.* 1.

MY DEAR H. G.,

I've been looking for you for days. So has all the Reform Club. I have been 'approached' with a request to 'approach' you on the matter of the correspondence between you and Henry James apropos of *Boon*.[1] Admirers and fanatics of H. J. regard his letters in this affair as the greatest statement of his artistic 'case' that he ever gave. In your place, if it pleased them, I would let them print the whole thing, without suppressing a phrase; and in fact there is only one short phase (about 'bad manners') to which any objection could be taken.[2] If they printed his letters (with the above-indicated suppression), and your replies, the matter would be perfect. Can't you agree to this, and content the vast H. J. world?

Yours

A. B.

[1] Bennett may well have been approached by Percy Lubbock, who was editing James's letters.

[2] The phrase Bennett refers to occurs in the first sentence of James's letter to Wells on 10 July 1915: "I am bound to tell you that I don't think your letter makes out any sort of case for the bad manners of *Boon*, so far as your indulgence in them at the expense of your poor old H.J. is concerned—I say 'your' simply because he has *been* yours, in the most liberal, continual, sacrificial, the most admiring and abounding critical way, ever since he began to know your writings: as to which you have had copious testimony." See *Henry James and H. G. Wells*, p. 265.

152

WELLS TO BENNETT

52 *St James's Court*
[25 *February* 1919.] *Buckingham Gate, S.W.* 1.

MY DEAR ARNOLD,

There is too much diplomacy about the James affair. Why don't the people come to me directly instead of pulling you in to the affair? I wrote carelessly in that correspondence, feeling I was dealing with an old man and being only anxious to propitiate him—without too much waste of epistolary effort on my part. The publication of the correspondence therefore as it stands might entirely misrepresent my attitude towards our "art." I kept no copy of my letters and have never given the matter ten minutes thought since.

Anyhow for various reasons I want to meet this Henry James cult face to face. There are several ragged ends want clearing and clipping in the affair.

So just ask whoever it is to deal directly with me.

Yours ever
H. G. WELLS

153

WELLS TO BENNETT

Easton Glebe,
Dunmow

[*October* 1919]

DEAR ARNOLD

That chap Cummings (Barbellion) [1] is on his beam ends financially and hasn't long to live. I think it would be kind if some of us were to guarantee his weekly expenses until he dies. He spends nearly £8 a week. He has to have a male attendant at £3.10.0. I'm suggesting that I pay 25/. a week to the end, that you do something of the same sort (you're not so deeply in it as I am), that Marsh does the like and perhaps one or two others and that Swinnerton is made treasurer and cashier. Will you come in?

Yours ever

H. G.

If so send a cheque to Swinny and tell him how much per week to pay out.

[1] Bruce Frederick Cummings (1889–1919), pseudonym W. N. P. Barbellion, a naturalist and journalist. Wells wrote the introduction to his *Journal of a Disappointed Man,* published in 1917 by Chatto & Windus, to whom Frank Swinnerton was reader.

154

WELLS TO BENNETT

[*November* 1919]
Easton Glebe,
Dunmow

DEAR ARNOLD

This is honour indeed. I have been at the *Outline of History* for more than a year of fanatical toil.

It is a thing of about 400,000 words. We shall never get on with our public life until we have a better historical foundation. I am trying to give something clear, true and *right*.

I am sending some uncorrected galleys and early illustrations in another envelope. This will show you the design and scale. Don't read em, just glance over them, but *please read* the INTRODUCTION. I will try to get to the club on Tuesday a little later than 1.15.

Yours ever

H. G.

155

BENNETT TO WELLS

12 *December* 1919

DEAR H. G.

I am still waiting for the free copies of the *History*. I make it a point of honour not to buy them. It may interest you to know that the opinion on the thing in Cambridge, where I have just been, is distinctly favourable.

By the way, a new Society for the study of education is being started under what seem to me to be very good auspices. It is being started by undergraduates at the said University, and you are wanted to inaugurate the thing by an appearance and a speech at the first meeting, which is to be important. I was requested to discover from you whether you would entertain the idea. I fancy that at the present stage you would get such a reception as no author has ever had from his contemporaries in this stone town built on a fen. Please let me know.

Yours,
A. B.

156

BENNETT TO MRS WELLS

12B George Street

22 *January* 1920   *Hanover Square W. 1.*[1]

DEAR LADY,

The more I read of H.G.'s *Outline* the more staggered I am by it. It is about the most useful thing of the kind

---

[1] A maisonette into which the Bennetts moved shortly after the war, although he retained Comarques until 1922.

ever done, and it is jolly well done. Full of imagination, and the facts assembled and handled in a masterly manner. But this letter is to tell *you* that I do think the proof-reading is very faulty. I don't care to seem to be always insisting to H. G. about details. I have no exaggerated idea of their importance, and I can keep the perspective as well as most folks. But these details *have* importance, and someone ought to see to them; because H. G. never will. Quite apart from numerous easily avoided verbal inelegancies, for which H. G. doesn't care one damn (but ought), there are positive mistakes, as in such phrases such as "as big or bigger than", and acute grammatical slips such as singular verbs after collective nouns which have a plural possessive pronoun. And so on. My impression is that the carelessnesses seem to come in patches. I would do the proofs myself, if he wanted, but I can't undertake a 500,000 word business.

I don't think the footnotes by friends ought to be signed only with initials, unless a table of footnote writers with full names is given at the beginning. And the famous phrase '*op. cit.*' (which many plain readers will not understand) ought never to be used for the same work on more than one page. The work ought to be re-cited on every page on which it is referred to.

How the fellow did the book in the time fair passes me. I cannot get over it. It's a life work.

Yours

A. B.

157

BENNETT TO MRS WELLS

11 *April* 1920

Comarques
Thorpe-le-Soken

DEAR LADY JANE,

Will you and H.G. be at Speech Day? I shall, but I don't think Marguerite will. Under the orders of Richard [1] I have written to a Mrs. Carmichael, from whom (he says) he has retained a room for me. Is this where you stay? I shall particularly object to eating by myself or with perfect strangers during my brief stay. Seldom have visitors come so far to stay so short as your two sons did the other day. They seemed to be in great form. I am $\frac{1}{2}$ way through Part XI.[2] He seems to have a fearful down on the Romans, but I rather think he is right. The Roman stuff is perhaps the best up to now. It is indeed fine. Especially Cato, Marius, and Co. It is a jolly sight more than a *vulgarisation* (French sound and sense) of history.

Yours

A. B.

P.S. The fellow's speech at the Newnes' dinner was A.1.[3]

[1] Richard Bennett. The Speech Day was held at Oundle School on 6 June.

[2] *The Outline of History* was issued in twenty-four fortnightly parts, November 1919–November 1920, by George Newnes Ltd.

[3] Newnes gave a dinner on 26 March in honour of *The Outline of History*, at which Wells spoke.

o

158

[Manuscript article by Bennett which does not appear to have been published]

MR. H. G. WELLS

Herbert George Wells has now been prominently before the reading public of the world for a quarter of a century. He began as a biologist; at the moment he stands forth as a universal historian; he has had dazzling successes as a prophet, but even so great a professor of divination as himself would hesitate to prophesy what will be his line of business ten years hence. His two chief characteristics are an eager willingness to learn—and to learn in public—and a tremendous, inexhaustible energy. His education has been conducted in the sight of nations, and in teaching others his most conspicuous feat has been to teach himself. Tennyson foresaw him when he sang that men rise on stepping-stones of their dead selves to higher things. As for his marvellous initiative energy, it is equally manifest in all his activities. Those who know him know that he is a terrific ball-player, using generally a game which he personally invented, but not averse from so traditional a pastime as hockey; that he will sweat his companions all day, argue with them all the evening on any and every political, philosophical, physiological and artistic question, put them to bed in collapse, and come down bright the next morning with the news that he has done several hours creative work in the middle of the night. To tell the briefness of the period in which he wrote his history of the world from 5,000,000 B.C. to A.D. 1920, in half a million words, would be to invite incredulity. It is conceivable that *The Outline of History* may dwarf all his other books, by the immensity of its scope and the mighty firmness of its grasp: for this reason we make no detailed reference to his numerous novels and other sociological productions. Mr. Wells admits—nay, proclaims—that he is highly dissatisfied with humanity and more than anything else wants to change it. Other and not lesser artists are in love with humanity and have a conviction that it cannot be changed.[1] But Mr. Wells would probably count himself as a preacher first and an artist second. That his achievements in both fields are astounding and admirable will be disputed by nobody.

[1] Cf. Joseph Conrad's words as reported in Hugh Walpole's journal on 23 January 1918: "His [Conrad's] final quarrel with Wells was: 'The difference between us, Wells, is fundamental. You don't care for humanity but think they are to be improved. I love humanity but know they are not!'" (*Hugh Walpole: A Biography* by Rupert Hart-Davis, 1952, p. 168.)

159
BENNETT TO MRS WELLS

12B George St.
31 *May* 1920   *Hanover Sq. W.*1

DEAR LADY JANE,

This is very thoughtful of you, and I am obliged. It is obvious that the breakfast must live in the memory of ten prefects. I will arrange commensurately. I will tell Mistress McM. to lay covers for 14.

It is illustrative of the superstitious faith of boys in the arrival of food that I had only heard of this breakfast in the vaguest way. I certainly had not been consulted.

I vote we stay till Monday.

It is understood between H. G. and me that we travel down to Bishops Stortford on Saturday by the 12 train together. But his estimate that we shall arrive at Oundle by 3 seems to me wildly optimistic.

Yours ever

A. B.

160

BENNETT TO WELLS

Comarques

15 *September* 1920   *Thorpe-le-Soken*

MY DEAR H. G.

Much obliged for the portly volume. I have kept regularly up to date with the parts, and am now in Part 22. Such reviews as I have seen are chiefly footling. I have never read a work with a greater sense of the *achievement* of the thing. In fact for the last 12 parts I have been in a state of perpetual amazement. The affair is handled; it is done; it is accomplished; the perspective is maintained, and there is an omnipresent feeling of masterliness. Anybody who knows what a work is, and what it means in labour, presence of mind, cerebration, and grit—especially on this immense scale—will regard congratulations as extremely inadequate. The book is a majestic success, both brilliant and solid. I regret the negligences of writing, but attach only the slightest importance to them. I think you were rather casual over the Renaissance; but I haven't much else in the way of animadversion. Nobody else on earth could have done the thing one tenth as well as you have done it. You have supplied a want, and made powerfully for righteousness.

Yours

A. B.

161

WELLS TO BENNETT

Easton Glebe,
[*October* 1920] *Dunmow*

DEAR E. A. B.

Your corrections gratefully accepted. The book [1] will be completely reprinted (with considerable correction) and with Horrabin's illustrations only by Cassells and sold for 18/– or £1 in one nice blue bound volume.

Note the statement that there is a Palaeolithic swastika is a howler.[2] The drawing in question was probably not earlier than 800 B.C. or at most 1000 B.C.

H. G.

[1] *The Outline of History,* 1920.
[2] In *The Outline of History* Wells had written, "The swastika is found in Palaeolithic bone drawings." (I, 84.) In the ninth revision of the edition Wells speaks of in this letter (*The Outline of History,* 1937, p. 140), the drawing remains, but there is no reference to Paleolithic bone drawings.

162

BENNETT TO MRS WELLS

12B *George Street*
8 *December* 1920   *Hanover Square, W*.1.

Dear Lady Jane,

The whole Jane world (extensive, orbicular) has been shaken to its depths by this affair of yours. Happily it now has reason to recover, and is recovering, and I am once more getting the limelight. Before your unhappy appearance in the pathological theatre, I was attracting a certain amount of attention by means of pyorrhea, high frequency electrical treatment, microbic injections, dentists, specialists, etc. But you wiped me off the map in one day. However, I think I can beat you in permanence of sickliness, and I am doubly glad of it. I saw H. G. yesterday. Dr. Shufflebotham,[1] who was there, predicted that he would have to stay at home today, and lo! so it is. He is immensely proud of the fact that he can make out cheques and pay bills without your help. In fact the entire club is much bored by his interminable recitals of feats in the cheque and payment line. You will have a horrible skein to unravel when you return to

[1] Dr. Frank Shuffllebotham, Bennett's friend and personal physician.

management. I hear you will be back for Christmas. It is the best news. We went to Edith Sitwell's reception last night. Crowds of poets, many of whom sat on the floor. Still, not tedious. The St. John Ervines were by standly. At least, *she* was. We are just beginning to know them. They are my sort. Tonight, Swedish ballet. Next week Actors Orphanage Fancy Dress Ball, C. Garden. Haven't been to one for ten years. This last week you have doubtless felt within you a peculiar but enheartening *in*fluence. You didn't know it, but it was the *e*ffluence of my blessing. I hope to see you frisking soon. Marguerite sends her love. Me too.

Yours ever

A. B.

163

WELLS TO BENNETT

Claridge's Hotel
Avenue des Champs-Elysées

[21 *January* 1921]   *Paris*

MY DEAR ARNOLD

I'm *en route* for Rome [1] and so far I've done very well
—a beautiful crossing and Paris like summer. I think I
shall get through to Amalfi all right and there a warm
hearted secretary will look after me night and day. I can't
help thinking of your motherly impulse in writing to me.
It showed a kindness and concern. And generally the
dear old *Reform* has been like a band of elder brothers
over my temporary hymenic indiscretions.

I'm really going to do nothing unpleasant or laborious
for two good months or more. Then I will come back
and be a credit to you.

And meanwhile dear Arnold

         I am

            Yours very gratefully

               H. G.

---

[1] Wells was beginning a two months' trip on the continent to
recover from the illness mentioned in the previous letter.

164

BENNETT TO WELLS

12*B George Street*
23 *May* 1921   *Hanover Square, W.* 1.

DEAR H. G.

Thanks for letting me see this pleasing document. The facts are that the discussion between Ray [1] and myself (in

---

[1] Ray Long, editor of *Cosmopolitan Magazine.* The document Bennett refers to follows, with Wells's comments.

[Typewritten]   *Savoy Hotel*
                                                 London
18 *May* 1921   *W.C.*2

Mr. H. G. Wells
    Eastern Gleb [*sic.*]
        Dunmow, Essex

DEAR MR. WELLS,

I am taking the liberty of writing to you from over here because Mr. Thorsen, business manager of *Cosmopolitan*, has suggested that in these days, when our affairs are so closely intertwined with those of the various European countries, you would be interested in knowing how the literary affairs on the two sides of the Atlantic are dove-tailing.

I have been making one of my regular trips to this side, because I share with Mr. Thorsen the view that the Editor of a magazine like *Cosmopolitan* is the real circulation manager; since we offer no premiums or other baits for circulation, the material the Editor puts in the publication is the sole factor which determines its sale. And the only way to get the worthwhile material is constantly to

the presence of Pinker and Swinnerton) turned solely on
the question of several stories, and the fellow gave me a
free hand. Nothing else happened and his account is an
ingenious falsification. I have done him 4 stories of which

---

go after it. I am prepared to travel any distance to get what I think
Cosmopolitan readers deserve.

Perhaps I can show you exactly what I mean by telling you about
Arnold Bennett. He is, as you know, one of the most graceful and
brilliant of living writers. But some of the stories he had delivered
to us recently seemed cold and stilted. I might have written him
a dozen letters without getting at the cause. But, over our coffee
at the Arts Club, it came out.

"Your enormous circulation frightens me," he said. "When
I think of writing for a million and a quarter buyers of a magazine—five million readers—I get stage fright."

[*In the margin beside the preceding paragraph Wells writes*: "Arnold!
Do we allow this sort of thing?"]

I explained to him that the reason Americans like his work is
because it is *his*, and he got the point immediately. And now he's
gone away to write real Arnold Bennett stories for *Cosmo* readers.

Winston Churchill, Secretary of State for the Colonies, and—
unless signs fail England's next Premier, has the feeling of the
American audience. [Marginal comment by Wells: "This to me."]
This may be because his mother was an American, but more likely
it is because he has travelled extensively in the States and made a
real study of us. It was amazing to me last Saturday, when we
lunched and spent the afternoon at his home, to see how instinctively he selected from some material he read me, the portions
which would be of greatest interest to Americans.

I have arranged, since coming over here, for *Cosmopolitan* to add
Robert Hichens, author of *The Garden of Allah*, to its list of distinguished English authors; we are to have first look at Joseph
Conrad's novel of the Napoleonic period; Mrs. C. N. Williamson
is searching for more articles as interesting as her word picture of

3 are A 1. I wouldn't defend the 4th. I have 2 to do, and in doing them I shall take him at his word, and there will be trouble.

Yours

A. B.

165

BENNETT TO WELLS

[Western Union Cablegram]

Arlington Hotel, Washington
11 *November* 1921

Well it's great stuff[1] continue.

ARNOLD

Monte Carlo; Cynthia Stockley is working on a novel of South Africa for us—and a dozen or more exceptional features are in the making.

An Editor has to be on the job much as a salesman has to keep out among his customers. That's why I'm over here—"calling on the trade," as Peter B. Kyne would say. And so far it has been a very successful trip. From here I go to Paris to see Robert W. Service, and arrange for more of those great poems of his; then home to the *Cosmopolitan* and little, old New York.

Sincerely yours

RAY LONG

[1] *Washington and the Hope of Peace*, 1922. Wells had accepted an offer to attend the Washington Conference as the special correspondent of the *New York World*. The twenty-nine articles in the book were printed in leading American and British newspapers from 7 November to 20 December 1921. Bennett probably read

166

BENNETT TO MRS WELLS

12B George Street

17 *November* 1922   *Hanover Square, W. 1.*

DEAR JANE

Nothing could suit me better, and I will come with the greatest pleasure and gratitude—unless (extremely improbably) I am called out of England. If this undesirable call should come I should know a considerable time in advance.

I was dining at honest John Galsworthy's last night. My God! He understands the art of life, that fellow does! I always thought my Duc di Montebello champagne was unequalled in the wide world: but his G. H. Mumm's

the articles in the *Daily Mail*. On the same date Frank Swinnerton wrote to Mrs Wells:

"Me and A. B.
Both agree
That you ought to ask A. B. and me
As a spree
To dinner (merely us three)
At yout F - L - A - T.
Verbum sat. sapient *i*
We think the articles of H. G.
From Washington Citee
Are deserving of the highest degree
(Or whatever it be)
Of celebritee."

Cordon Rouge 1911 was *marvellous*. I had too much,[1]
but am working as usual this morning.

After my brief conversation with H. G. yesterday I
have called off the secretaryship.

Yours ever

A. B.

167

BENNETT TO MRS WELLS

75 *Cadogan Square*[2]

25 *May* 1923   *S.W.* 1.

MY DEAR JANE,

Many thanks, but I shall join the yacht on the 31st for
the summer. So that with regret I must refuse.

No I have not in the least disappeared. I am revolving
just as usual. In order to see F.S.[3] I have had to *go* and

[1] According to Dorothy Cheston Bennett a statement such as
this meant, at the most, two glasses.

[2] Bennett moved to this "rather noble thing in houses" in
December 1922.

[3] Frank Swinnerton had recently moved to Old Tokefield,
Cranleigh, Surrey, a cottage converted from three small seven-
teenth-century cottages and modernized. He wrote to Mrs Wells
on 31 May, "A. B. has been down to see the cottage, and bumped
his head. *That* taught him! He looked all over the place with a
critical eye, and I heard him mutter '*Very* interesting to see other
people's ideas.'"

see him in his rural wigwam. Do you think *he* would
have done as much? I do not think!

Ever yours

A. B.

P.S. *Men Like Gods* [1] is *very fine*. And this is the view of
all its readers that I have met with. AB
P.S. No. I had not forgotten. Are you coming to the
yacht this season? Or not? AB

168

WELLS TO BENNETT

4, *Whitehall Court*

(*Flat* 120)

1 *November* 1923   *S.W.* 1.

DEAR ARNOLD

I have to join the chorus. *Riceyman Steps* [2] is a great
book. I hate to go back on an old friend but I think it is
as good or better than *The Old Wives' Tale*. It's simpler
and shorter but one does not judge books by weight.

Yours ever

H. G.

[1] 1923. But Bennett wrote to Dorothy Cheston Bennett: "I
have received D. H. Lawrence's new stories which appear to be
very fine, and Wells's new novel [*Men Like Gods*] of which I have
my doubts." *Arnold Bennett, a Portrait Done at Home* (1935),
p. 177.
[2] 1923.

169

WELLS TO BENNETT

5 *November* 1923　　　　　　　　4, *Whitehall Court*

BELOVED ARNOLD

Let's gossip somewhere. I leave the choice to you.
The thing is that it will be pleasant to talk together again.

Yours ever

H. G.

170

BENNETT TO WELLS

21 *November* 1923　　　　　　　75, *Cadogan Square*

MY DEAR H. G.

Look here; this is very disturbing, and ought to be
seen to.[1] All pleasure places are more or less "off" and
rainy in December. Cintra is in a hollow of the hills between the Estorils. Marvellous in spring, but not much
till then. Very mild, though. Wonderful view from the
castle over the town. Trains: A train. Country south-

---

[1] Wells was ill and he was also exhausted by his second unsuccessful political campaign as Labour candidate for London
University. For his description of his feeling of discontent and
futility, see *Experiment in Autobiography*. (II, 737 ff.)

ward hilly; northward flat. All public services absolutely rotten. I think you might get bored there, but you
wouldn't be cold there. If I were you I should go by
steamer direct to South Italy; or, if that is too far, to
Toulon, and go into the hills north of there. This is
surely the least fatiguing way of travel for an infirm person. If you decide on Cintra the Booth Line is the line,
to Lisbon. (I'll tell George Booth to cosset you if you
like.) Small steamers, but very well run. St. Jean
Estoril near the mouth of the Tagus is very agreeable as
a centre but all the Estorils are a bit spoilt by the architecture of profiteers—totally fantastic and horrid. Devil-
ish cold in the mornings. But sun.

What's up with Tangier or Tunis? Nothing except the
French ships that take you across the Mediterranean.

When you come through London let me know and I
hope you'll *let* people look after you.

Yours ever anxious

A. B.

P

171

WELLS TO BENNETT

Easton Glebe,

21 *November* 1923   *Dunmow*

DEAR ARNOLD.

Thanks for the tips. I think I may go on to Madeira straight and back via Lisbon. I've got a hell of a cold on the top of a wheezy lung but nothing excessively grave. I shall try and do a long promised meeting next week and then warm up before I start. I may stick it here over Xmas. I shall go alone because R. is having the time of her life in America and I don't want to interrupt it.

Are there people to talk to round and about Lisbon?

Yours ever

H. G.

172

BENNETT TO WELLS

23 *November* 1923   75 *Cadogan Square*

MY DEAR H. G.,

Why the meeting? It must be a strain on the heart, and if you have got anything that predisposes to pneumonia you want all the heart you can summon. I am seriously told that "Yahdil" is a *specific* for pneumonia and such things. Yes, there are people to talk to at Lisbon. The Jaynes, for instance. He is a son of the Bishop of Chester, and partner in one of the chief importing firms there, and in close touch with the Booth Line. Mrs. Jayne is an agreeable piece, to whom you would be meat and drink. There is also a fellow named Edgar Prestage, who used to be on the *Morning Post*. I can fix these things up for you if you like. Also George Booth. I've never been to Madeira, but I'm told its a very lugubrious place to *stay* at. You would want to fit in your steamers, and the sooner the better. I think these steamers are usually pretty full. Consider me at your disposition in all things.

Yours
A. B.

173

BENNETT TO MRS WELLS

18 *December* 1923   75 *Cadogan Square*

MY DEAR JANE,

Of course this is to thank you very much for your kind care: which I do. But *really* it's to annoy you by telling you that I *have* had a letter, and a long letter, and an intimate letter full of strange details, from your Swinney.[1]

[1] Frank Swinnerton went to the United States in November 1923 for a three-months lecture tour.

I had to "go behind" last night after the show.[1]
Home at 12:45, and I was scarce in bed when someone
rang me up!

       Neuralgia all gone. Fatigue omnipresent.
       Elizabeth's ball tonight!
       Good God!

              Love to all
                Yours
                  A. B.

174

BENNETT TO WELLS

14 *May* 1924   75 *Cadogan Square*

MY DEAR H. G.

I beg to state that *The Dream* [2] has held me throughout. (I didn't read it before, as I was travelling in Spain
with Max B.[3] He, however, *did* read it in trains and it
held him too, and he spoke very highly of it.) I disagree
with the élite who say that there is too much framework.
On the contrary I think there isn't enough and that what

[1] Probably at the Kingsway Theatre, where Dorothy Cheston
was playing Viola in *Twelfth Night*. In his *Journal* Bennett noted
on 27 December: "Kingsway Theatre. 'Twelfth Night.' . . . I enjoyed it more than the other two performances which I had seen.
Then we went behind to Dorothy Cheston's room, and heard
about things."

[2] *The Dream*, 1924, first printed serially in *Nash's and Pall Mall
Magazine*, October 1923 to May 1924.

[3] William Maxwell Aitken, Lord Beaverbrook.

there is isn't complex enough. I say naught of the super-
élite who have discovered that the book would be better
without any framework at all! Good God! My boy, this
is a very good and a disturbing book, as to which I am
enthusiastic. (So are others.) And may God keep us all!
It is about time you and I met. And I think Swinny
might meet us too. He is very interesting and funny
about U.S.A., and not spoilt by his triumphs. Love to all.

Thine
A. B.

175

BENNETT TO WELLS

1 *June* 1924   75 *Cadogan Square*

MY DEAR H. G.,

   Well, 2 unfortunates have been pushed out of the stalls
into the dress circle for you. The tickets will await you
at the box-office; but there is bound to be a great crush at
the box-office before the performance, and if I were you
I should send up for them in advance. You will have to
pay for them. Drury Lane is run by a "Board."[1] I have
had to pay for some of my own seats. Please understand
that this play is merely a *tactful* attempt to break with
Drury Lane traditions and to seduce the Board. The

---

[1] The play referred to here is *A London Life*, written by Bennett
in collaboration with Edward Knoblock, which turned out to be
a failure.

latter part of the attempt has already failed. Not a single member of the board (except Dean) [1] believes in the play, and one of them is so certain of failure that he has resigned in advance.

Thine

A. B.

176

WELLS TO BENNETT

Easton Glebe

20 *October* 1924   *Dunmow*

DEAR ARNOLD

I have been reading (with admiration and delight) in *Elsie and the Child*.[2] This morning I found in my press cuttings this. I am amused. Have you ever met X.Y.? She does not like "Last Love." For sheer unadulterated skill 'The Paper Cap' makes me bow. You are the master craftsman. There is no one like you.

Yours ever

H. G.

[1] Basil Dean, joint managing director of the Theatre Royal, Drury Lane 1924–25, and producer of *A London Life*.

[2] *Elsie and the Child, a tale of Riceyman Steps, and other Stories*, 1924. The titles mentioned later in the letter are stories in this volume. "Last Love" concerns a spinster of thirty-nine who falls in love with a man of twenty-five. "The Paper Cap" is the story of a wealthy bachelor who finds that even a yacht cannot protect him from the vulgarity of London Society.

177

BENNETT TO WELLS

23 *October* 1924   75 *Cadogan Square*

MY DEAR H. G.

This is good news to me, and I rejoice (humbly). I know X.Y. She now has a complex—result of the death of her fiancé in the war. She is drying up, and I am sorry for her. She was probably always a cat. I remember that she said some laudatory things, among a lot of slanging, in a review of one of my books in *Time and Tide*. Some readers weighed in with abuse of *her* for giving me any praise. Whereupon she withdrew her praise, saying she hadn't meant it. I am always fighting against the proverb: "All women are alike." But there is a damned lot of truth in it.

McBride, Lankester and Salter are my men.[1]

Sorry you can't come tonight.

Thine

A. B.

P.S. Your letter was addressed "78" and took 3 days to reach me.

[1] Probably Ernest William MacBride (1866–1940), eminent British zoologist. Sir Arthur (later Lord) Salter (b. 1881), an economist, was at this time a member of the advisory council of the League of Nations. Sir Edwin Ray Lankester, as we have noted previously, was, like MacBride, a leading zoologist.

178

BENNETT TO WELLS

9 September 1925 75 *Cadogan Square*

MY DEAR H. G.

I don't know where you are. Temple[1] told me he thought you had left England.[2] I've read *C. A.'s Father*,[3] for the copy of which my thanksgivings. I think it is a very fine moral allegory or parable, and full of meat for people who want everything to be done in a fortnight. I might call it a bit over-cruel, but I don't mind that. We don't have $\frac{1}{2}$ enough cruelty in novels. C. A. is very good (and very naughty). Curious mixture of romance and realism! I think the book will hold people.

[*One paragraph omitted by request of the Public Trustee.*]

Thine

A. B.

[1] Richmond Temple, at this time publicity director for the Savoy Hotel chain.

[2] After Wells's retreat from London in January 1924, he travelled on the Continent, finally establishing a second home at Lou Bastidon near Grasse, where he spent most of the following three winters.

[3] Wells's *Christina Alberta's Father*, 1925.

179

BENNETT TO MRS WELLS

17 *September* 1925   75 *Cadogan Square*

MY DEAR JANE,

This was very disturbing news about Frank.[1] I hadn't the least idea he'd been ill. Remember me to him. I suppose there is no sort of doubt, now, that he has come through. But these things are terrible while they are on. You have all my retrospective sympathy. I was once nearly dead myself once, and very annoyed about it.

I noticed strangely few misprints in *C. A's Pa*, though I had my malicious eye open for them. I like Preemby better than Lewisham, Kipps or Mr. Polly. He is a very distinguishedly-conceived character. The book is urbane.

Well, I like Frank much: but then I am much attached to the whole H. G. family. Thank H. G. for his letter, and yourself for your kind message to Dorothy. She is 34, and a very hefty wench.

Ever yours,

A. B.

[1] Wells's son, Frank Richard.

180

BENNETT TO MRS WELLS

Winter Palace
Menton, A M
1 *March* 1926   *France*

MY SWEET JANE,

This is most nice of you and H. G. Only we shan't be in London until March 21st anyhow, and moreover Dorothy will not be in a very going-out mood then. So we couldn't accept. I shall be 'about' after Mch 21st or so. I think we shall stay at Claridges for a week or so until Dorothy goes into retirement. I hope you'll call. Good about H. G.'s novel.[1] I finished my long novel Jan 26th [2] and I began another one shortly afterwards and have written one-sixth of it already.[3] Dorothy is very well. Me too. We leave here next Sabbath and go by easy stages to Paris and thence to Calais and London. She must travel slowly. All is well, except that my youngest brother is dying of consumption in North Wales. He is 49 or so.

---

[1] Probably *The World of William Clissold*, published in three volumes, 1926.

[2] *Lord Raingo*, 1926.

[3] Probably *The Strange Vanguard*, a fantasia, published in book form in 1928.

We have had, on the whole, simply marvellous weather (8 weeks in Rome). Dorothy conveyeth love unto you.

Ever yours

A. B.

P.S. Respex to the Franklet.

181

BENNETT TO WELLS

Amberley

1 *June* 1926 *Sussex*

DEAR H. G.

I know nothing except that Pinker wrote and asked me if I could do a 3 or 4,000 word synopsis for a payment (presumably on account of royalties) of £2,000 on delivery. I said I would. This was last Friday. I haven't even had the draft contract yet.

We are expecting you and Jane to lunch or tea here soon.

Thine

A. B.

182

BENNETT TO WELLS

27 *October* 1926   75 *Cadogan Square*

MY DEAR H. G.,

Thy letter is most impressive and appreciated, and I am full of satisfaction therein and thank thee. I meant to unfold myself the other night about *Clissold II*.[1] I was, as thou knowest, firmly held and much impressed by *Clissold I*. But *Clissold II* is decidedly better. The women are very well done indeed and it is all keyed up more, livelier, more resilient than *C I*, which nevertheless had the qualities denoted by the above adjectives. This is an *original* novel. My novels never are.

Thine ever

A. B.

183

BENNETT TO MRS WELLS

16 *November* 1926   75 *Cadogan Square*

MY SWEET JANE,

I'd meant to send you a note far far sooner, but God willed otherwise. Like yours, my life is terrible—and

[1] *The World of William Clissold*, volume II.

like Dorothy's.[1] All I wanted to say was that our week-
end with you was *very* agreeable and that you made your
good-nature and kindliness *felt*—and that I was captious
as usual. What a pity I am like that, isn't it? Easton G.
is a great tonic. We think of going to Cortino (ci-devant
Austrian, now Italian). But nothing is sure. The A.
Huxleys are there and will be there for a year. I hear
good of it. We should go between Xmas and the N. Y.

Ever your devoted

A. B.

184

WELLS TO BENNETT [*Postcard*]

[21 *July* 1927]

I shall be at the Malthusian Dinner on the 26th and
motoring home on the morning of the 27th. Very delighted if I can give you a lift down.

H. G.

---

[1] Bennett was extremely busy at this time. He was very active
on the Board of Management of the Lyric Theatre, Hammersmith;
he was planning a novel, *Accident*; he was attending rehearsals of
Riceyman Steps at the Ambassadors' Theatre. All this was in addition to his normal schedule of social and journalistic activities.

185

BENNETT TO WELLS

Royal Victoria Hotel

30 *July* 1927   *St Leonards-on-Sea*

MY DEAR H. G.,

I enclose the reply from Roche.[1] All I will say is that I talked with him for 2 hours, that he made a very favorable impression on me, and that despite the unavoidable 'convulsion' etc., if I was in your place I should try him. The treatment is purely medicinal. In a general confession, he told me his charges when I saw him. I think he has a very large practice; he lives very modestly, and I should say that he is saving a lot of money. I should be surprised if he isn't a Jew.

If you decide not to try him, please return his letter to me, and I will suitably deal with it.

Our loves to Jane

Thine

A. B.

---

[1] Raphael Roche, who claimed to have a cure, or at least a very effective palliative, for cancer and other serious diseases. Roche was being consulted on behalf of Mrs Wells, who was dying of cancer.

186

BENNETT TO WELLS

2 *August* 1927

Royal Victoria Hotel
St Leonards-on-Sea

DEAR H. G.

Yes, of course. I quite appreciate your position. But mine also must be clear. Assuming that I ask Roche for satisfactory evidence, he gives it, shall you consult him? I don't want to make him feel awkward.

Loves to Jane

Thine

A. B.

187

BENNETT TO WELLS

11 *August* 1927

Royal Victoria Hotel
St Leonards-on-Sea

MY DEAR H. G.

I enclose a letter from Roche.[1] I assume that you will follow this up.

Love to Jane

Yours

A. B.

[1] Bennett encloses a letter from Roche which gives the name and address of the brother of a woman whom Roche's *Science of Curative Medicine* had kept alive, Roche claims, for two or three years after her doctor had predicted immediate death from cancer. In a marginal note Wells directs his secretary to send a letter to the brother.

188

BENNETT TO MRS WELLS

Hotel Adlon

14 *September* 1927 *Berlin*

MY DEAR JANE,

Instead of coming to see you I went to Berlin with Beaverbrook, Diana Cooper, and Venetia Montague.[1] And here I am, after a mad 4 days. I'm starting home tomorrow. We came by a Hamburg-America liner,—Southampton–Cuxhaven, and we return by a Hamburg-American liner Cuxhaven–Bologne. Great fun. Next week I hope to come and see you. Dorothy is so completely absorbed in her Court Theatre scheme that she could not leave London for one day.[2]

Ever your devoted

A. B.

[1] This party also included Lord Castlerosse. Lady Diana Cooper, as Lady Diana Manners, had appeared as the Madonna in Max Reinhardt's *The Miracle*. Venetia Montagu was The Hon. Mrs Edwin Montagu.

[2] The Bennetts and Theodore Komisarjevsky had formed Sloane Productions Co. Ltd to produce plays at the Court Theatre. The second play was *Mr. Prohack*, produced by Dorothy Cheston Bennett, who also acted in it. It ran from 16 November 1927 to 7 January 1928, when the lease was up and no other theatre was available.

189

BENNETT TO WELLS

27 September 1927   75 *Cadogan Square*

MY DEAR H. G.

I wrote to Page[1] on Sunday, as his attendances at the Reform are irregular. However, he came yesterday and I was there in case, and he at once agreed. He said he assumed he would see and approve the form beforehand: but I had already assured him of this in my letter. He said: "I am very old, and the emotion may be too much for me." On this point I comforted him. He said he would write to you. In case he doesn't his address is Woodcote, Godalming. Let me know if I can be useful in any way.

Thine

A. B.

[1] T. E. Page (1850–1936), classical scholar, teacher, editor and political critic, noted for his commanding personality and, on special occasions, his oratory. He delivered the address, prepared by Wells, at Mrs Wells's funeral on 10 October 1927.

Q

190

BENNETT TO WELLS

22 November 1927   75 *Cadogan Square*

MY DEAR H. G.

A week or two before he died Charlie Masterman [1] wrote a pencil memorandum (I've seen it) in which he suggested that in case of death or insanity certain of his friends (you among them) might be asked to consider the question of the education of his children. There are three children: Margaret 17, Neville 15, and Dorothy 13. First two said to have much talent.

A close connection of the family, Reginald Bray (son of late Lord Bray) with a reputation for practical sagacity and knowledge of affairs, has gone into the matter, and he estimates that if about £4,000 were raised now, it would suffice to finish the education of all three children in the manner Charlie strongly desired. The fund would be put into an ad hoc trust.

Do you feel like contributing? There are 8 or 10 names.

Mrs. Masterman will have just enough to live on (about

---

[1] C. F. G. Masterman (1873–1927), former Liberal Cabinet minister. When he was dying he told his wife, "If you're really in a hole, go to 'A. B.' He's the one." (Pound, p. 325.)

£350 p. a., it is hoped) provided she earns something by her pen, as she will.

I've had a long talk with her.

Hommages à Madame.[1]

Yours

A. B.

191

BENNETT TO WELLS

20 *December* 1927   75 *Cadogan Square*
MY DEAR H. G.,

The Charles affair is now in order and the money all promised. Will you kindly therefore weigh in with the amount you suggested? I shall be grateful.

Thine

A. B.

192

BENNETT TO WELLS

28 *December* 1927   75 *Cadogan Square*
MY DEAR H. G.

Many thanks for the cheque. I enclose formal receipt.

I will let you know very soon about my coming down. I cannot decide until some theatrical business is settled.

Thine

A. B.

[1] Odette Keun.

[Enclosure]

Received of Mr. H. G. Wells the sum of Fifty Pounds contribution to the Masterman Educational Trust Fund.

ARNOLD BENNETT

28 *February* 1927

193

BENNETT TO WELLS

1 *February* 1928   75 *Cadogan Square*

DEAR H. G.

Is it true that Madame Odette is ill? I want to know, as I am very much concerned for you.

Yours

A. B.

194

BENNETT TO WELLS

28 *June* 1928   75 *Cadogan Square*

MY DEAR H. G.,

In great haste. Just preparing to flit. I had already signed the letter and returned it when your communication came. I think that there can be no doubt that the Government has been remiss in this matter. As for

Gorell, of course he only signs because he is now chairman of the Authors' Society.[1]

In returning the letter to Thring I complained of the composition of the same. If he does not do something about that I will rebel. I will also say to him that I have only signed on the understanding that the other people he mentioned to me all signed. But you cannot possibly keep Gorell out of it. Indeed he *ought* to sign.

I return Thring's letter to you.

Thine
A. B.

195

WELLS TO BENNETT

614 St. Ermin's

5 *October* 1928 [Postmark]   *Westminster*

Mysterious letter from an unknown correspondent.

    [*Enclosure*]   H. G.

It was a dispicable thing you did a few months ago. Henry. I had the pleasure of meeting Mr. Bennett many years ago at Clevedon Somerset.[2]

---

[1] The reason for this complaint by Wells against the Authors' Society is obscure. Wells apparently had thought Lord Gorell was attempting to use his office as chairman of the society to enhance his literary prestige. G. Herbert Thring was secretary of the Authors' Society.

[2] Apparently a "crank" letter. There is no record of the "dispicable thing" referred to.

196

WELLS TO BENNETT

24 *October* 1928

614 St. Ermin's
Westminster

DEAR ARNOLD.

I see your serial in the *Film Weekly*. I have a dispute arising about the custom of the trade and the publication of film synopses. Is this serial a "synopsis"? Is your publication of it as a serial entirely independent of the cinema film transaction? There seems some slight danger that synopses written by us may be published as serials without our consent and to the detriment of legitimate serials.

Yours ever

H. G.

197

BENNETT TO WELLS

25 *October* 1928

MY DEAR H. G.,

The publication of *Piccadilly* is entirely independent of the film transaction, as I kept all the publishing rights except the right to publish a synopsis not exceeding 2000 words. My scenario is 16,000 words. I am, however, having a row with the *Film Weekly* editor this very day because he has completely concealed the fact that the thing is a film-scenario, and is starting it as my "new story". I may add a postscript after I have seen the fellow.

Thine

A. B.

P.S. I have seen him and he has given in, and is to state in each future instalment that it is the scenario of a film now being produced by Dupont.

198

WELLS TO BENNETT

Lou Pidou [1]

Saint Mathieu

Grasse, A.-M.

6 *May* 1929

DEAR ARNOLD

I like *The Religious Interregnum* [2] because it is you, but I don't agree for a moment about the Ethics of Jesus. I don't believe in non-resistance and I found the whole code unstimulating and inconsistent [ink blot] (*What* a fountain pen and *what* blotting paper!) Ethics of meek manners and economic inactivity (consider the lilies) with the

---

[1] Wells had moved into Lou Pidou from Lou Bastidon in the spring of 1927.

[2] 1929.

smug satisfaction of knowing what happened to Dives in the back of one's mind. No. Give me magnanimity but not non-resistance to evil.

Yours ever

H. G.

199

BENNETT TO WELLS

19 *October* 1929   *75 Cadogan Square*

DEAR H. G.,

I am very sorry that it is quite impossible for me to come to your dinner. All I have to say to you now is that I share the views generally prevailing among members of the Editorial Board of the *Realist*.[1] In my opinion the Editorial Board has done its work very well indeed. The members have given a considerable amount of time to the enterprise, and some of them have written articles at prices far below the value of those articles in the market.

[1] *The Realist, A Journal of Scientific Humanism*, began monthly publication with Major Archibald Church as general editor in April 1929, and continued until January 1930. The editorial board included Wells, Bennett, Harold J. Laski, Aldous and Julian Huxley, and Rebecca West. As early as July, however, the magazine ran into financial difficulty. The editor and editorial board believed that they had received a commitment from Lord Melchett (Alfred Moritz Mond), Chairman of Imperial Chemical Industries Ltd., for financial backing and management for a period of at least two years. This aid was not forthcoming, however, and the magazine ceased publication after ten issues.

That would have been perfectly all right if the financial side of the affair had been properly managed. It is unnecessary to criticise in detail the activities of the Business Board. And I would not say that the majority of the members of the Business Board are to blame. The results of the activities of the Business Board are notorious. Obligations have not been met. Contributors and members of the staff have not been paid, and members of the Editorial Board have received angry and abusive letters from these creditors. The good name of the members of the Editorial Board has been seriously compromised. At any rate I know that mine has. Members of the Editorial Board went into the *Realist* in the belief and on the assurance that the resources and the business methods of a great business organisation were behind it. They have been deceived. Neither the resources nor the methods of the big organisation have been forthcoming, and there appears to be no sign of their forthcoming. Letters have not been answered. Appeals have been ignored. Bills have been left unpaid, and chaos reigns. To argue that the Editorial Board has nothing to do with the business side would be preposterous.[1] The editorial and business sides are inseparable. Without the name of Lord Melchett the *Realist* could not have been started at all. Lord Melchett has probably had no active part whatever in the affair. He may be ignorant of the present

[1] Handwritten note by Wells: "I don't agree as regards liability."

state of affairs. In any case I think that he ought to be plainly informed of what the present state of affairs is. I am in favour of the most drastic action.

Yours

A. B.

200

BENNETT TO WELLS

1 *February* 1930   75 *Cadogan Square*

MY DEAR HERBERT GEORGE,

I hear that Jo Davidson is going to meet you and do your bust.[1] This is merely to certify that he is a good friend of mine, and I anticipate that you will like him. His wife too is A 1, but invalidish. I am still struggling with my long book,[2] which has been rather snowed under by Dorothy's new (successful) revival of *Milestones*. *You* try and write a book while your mate is producing a play of yours! And see!

Hommages affectueux à Madame Odette

Thine

A. B.

[1] George Doran, of Doubleday, Doran & Co., commissioned the American sculptor Jo Davidson to make busts of Wells, Bennett and ten other English authors "for the perfectly legitimate purposes of a fresh presentation of your work and you to the great public in America." (Doran to Wells, 14 December 1929.) Davidson went down to Grasse for the sittings in February 1930. The plaster bust was completed and photographed but apparently never cast in bronze.   [2] *Imperial Palace.*

201

WELLS TO BENNETT

Villa Aurora
64A Boulevard D'Italie

10 *February* 1930   *Monte Carlo*

DEAR ARNOLD,

You know how these things happen and just what weight to attach to them.[1]

And I am yours ever,

H. G. with love from Odette.

---

[1] Dear Mr. Bennett,

My new book of reminiscences *As I Knew Them* will be out on the 28 Feb: and no doubt the review copies will be delivered a week earlier (Hutchinson's).

I am asking "H. G."—with whom I lunched at Lou Pidou the other day, to put in a good word for me with you, because what you say in the *Evening Standard* simply makes a book.

They are only sketches of people I have known, and it doesn't pretend to be "superior" in any way. Max Beerbohm gives the book his blessing but he hasn't read it!

Yours very sincerely
ELLA HEPWORTH DIXON

202

BENNETT TO WELLS

17 *February* 1930   75 *Cadogan Square*

Mr Arnold Bennett has much pleasure in accepting Mr. H. G. Wells's kind invitation for Friday March 7th at 8 o'clock.

203

WELLS TO BENNETT

Lou Pidou
Saint Mathieu

28 *February* 1930   *Grasse, A.-M.*

Dear E. A. B.

This rather hard-minded young man has been known to me for years.[1] I think this is not bad plain description of a social atmosphere. Anyhow he begs me to send it to you and as I've written him a word of praise myself, I can hardly refuse.

Yours ever

H. G.

[1] Wells is sending Bennett a novel called *Dear England* by Eric N. Simons. In a letter to Wells, 20 February, Simons wrote: "You were good enough to offer to send a copy of my book to Arnold Bennett with a personal note. I hope A. B. will like it. I have taken the liberty of inscribing it to him."

204

BENNETT TO WELLS

10 *March* 1930   75 *Cadogan Square*

MY DEAR H. G.

For your information I enclose copy of a letter which I have today sent to the Chairman of the Society of Authors.[1]

Yours ever

A. B.

P.S. The 'personal postscript' referred to in my letter to Gorell was written in Gorell's own hand, and ran as follows: "I might add that we have every hope of settling by arbitration the unfortunate dispute in question."

A. B.

205

WELLS TO BENNETT

614 *St. Ermin's*
11 *March* 1930   *Westminster*

DEAR ARNOLD.

Just the chastening words required. Many thanks for bothering about this case—and relieving my bother.

Yours ever

H. G. W.

[1] Appendix C, p. 277.

206

WELLS TO BENNETT

614 St. Ermin's

27 *March* 1930   *Westminster*

DEAR ARNOLD

Touching it is to read over those letters.[1] What a good friendship it has been! What a good friend you have been! I've sent them all on to Geoffrey West, who will be found dead under his accumulations 'of material.' God knows what he will make of it all!

Yours ever

H. G.

207

WELLS TO BENNETT

47 Chiltern Court
Clarence Gate

25 *September* 1930   *N.W.*1

DEAR ARNOLD

Can you lunch with me here on Friday 3rd? Please. At **1.15.**

Yours ever

H. G.

[1] Wells is apparently referring to his own letters to Bennett. Geoffrey West used Wells's letters to Bennett in his biography of Wells (1930), but no letters from Bennett to Wells.

208

WELLS TO BENNETT

124 Quai D'Auteuil
Paris XVI

7 October 1930

Arnold you are a dear. You are the best friend I've
ever had. This may colour my vision. I don't think
it does. We are also contemporary writers and that alone
ought to keep us clear headed about each other. But this
big book of yours seems to me a really great book.[1] I've
read it with much the same surprise and delight that I felt
about *The Old Wives' Tale*. It's amazingly complete.
It's your complete conquest of a world you've raided time
after time—not always to my satisfaction. It's an immense picture of a social phase and there is not a character
in it that isn't freshly observed true to type and individual—so far as I can check you. Gracie I thought began
a little too splendid but that comes all right in the
ensemble. I agree with the thesis of the increasing
"secondariness" of women. I've tried that myself in
Clissold and *The Secret Places of the Heart*.[2] The women

[1] *Imperial Palace*, 1930.

[2] In both *The World of William Clissold* (1926) and *The Secret
Places of the Heart* (1922) Wells's protagonists find women able to
support, but not partake of, a dedicated man's life-work. Social and
technological advances—protection of the young, household con-
veniences, for example—have intensified the "secondariness" of
the great majority of women, by relieving them of their traditional
duties, although Wells sees in the future a select class of highly

won't like you. You get something of the opposite feeling in *Harriet Hume*: [1] the essential fact of the story is
the same. May Flower [2] do his duty by you.

Yours ever,

H. G.

209

BENNETT TO WELLS

15 *November* 1930   97 *Chiltern Court* [3]

MY DEAR H. G.

I return your key herewith. All our thanks. Dorothy
is very grateful to you, and she was more comfortable up
there than she would have been anywhere else. She was
exhausted before she came here and had been complaining
of sleeplessness for weeks. Also she is now very worried
about her part, which she took against my advice.[4] The

gifted women sharing the work and aspirations of equally gifted
men. In *Imperial Palace* Evelyn Orcham finds the beautiful and
intelligent Gracie Savott unwilling to share his love for her with his
dedication to his hotel. The similarity between the books is a broad
one, however. Evelyn Orcham has little of the mystic consecration
of William Clissold or Sir Richmond Hardy.

[1] By Rebecca West, published in 1926. Harriet Hume, to over-
simplify, represents the good and the altruistic in the life of Arnold
Conderex. In turning his back on her for worldly success in politics, he brings about his own moral destruction.

[2] Newman Flower, of Cassell & Company, who published
Imperial Palace.

[3] The Bennetts moved here from 75 Cadogan Square in October 1930.

[4] Dorothy Cheston Bennett had a minor part, that of Miss
Cecelia Flinders, in *The Man from Blankley's* by F. Anstey, which

producing is rotten and was bound to be. Her mother died this morning at 10.55.

Yours
A. B.

210

BENNETT'S SECRETARY TO WELLS

17 *February* 1931   97 *Chiltern Court*

DEAR MR. WELLS,

Mr. Arnold Bennett is still too ill to see any correspondence, but I read your card to him and he asks me to thank you for writing and sends his love to you both.

Mr. Bennett does not know it, but he has typhoid and not influenza. Only one or two people are being told what the illness really is, as the doctors do not want Mr. Bennett to know, and it has been kept out of the press. He is slightly better today, and the doctors were very pleased with him this morning. It will be about another fortnight before there is any definite improvement, and he is of course forbidden all visitors.[1]

Yours faithfully
WINIFRED NERNEY
Secretary

---

was revived at the Fortune Theatre on 26 November 1930. It was the initial production of the People's Theatre movement, designed to provide London with good plays at popular prices.

[1] Arnold Bennett died at Chiltern Court on 27 March 1931.

R

APPENDIX A

BENNETT'S REVIEW OF *THE INVISIBLE MAN*

"The Invisible Man"

Like most of Mr. H. J. [*sic*] Wells's novels and stories, this tale is based upon an Idea—the Idea that a man by a scientific process can make himself invisible. The Idea is not a new one—I think I have met with it several times before—but it is worked with an ingenuity, a realism, an inevitableness, which no previous worker in the field of "grotesque romance," has ever approached, and which surpasses in some respects all Mr. Wells's former efforts. The strength of Mr. Wells lies in the fact that he is not only a scientist, but a most talented student of character, especially quaint character. He will not only ingeniously describe for you a scientific miracle, but he will set down that miracle in the midst of a country village, sketching with excellent humour the inn-landlady, the blacksmith, the chemist's apprentice, the blacksmith, [*sic*] the doctor, and all the other persons whom the miracle affects. He attacks you before and behind, and the result is that you are compelled to yield absolutely to his weird spells.

The Invisible Man thought he was going to do great things when he devisualised himself (he did, in fact, terrorise a whole district), but he soon found his sad error, and his story is one of failure, growing more pathetic and grimmer as it proceeds; the last few pages are deep tragedy, grotesque but genuine. The theme is developed in a masterly manner. The history of the man's first hunt in London for clothes and a mask wherewith to hide his invisibility, is a farce dreadful in its significance, but this is nothing to the naked, desperate tragedy of his last struggle against visible mankind. Indeed, the latter half of this book is pure sorrow. The invisible man is no longer grotesque, but human. One completely loses sight of the merely wonderful aspect of the phenomena in watching the dire pathos of his loneliness in a peopled world. Mr. Wells has achieved poetry.

Although the book contains the best work the author has done, it is not free from slight blemish. Mr. Wells seems to be losing his affectionate care for the minutiæ of style, a surprising lapse in a man trained under W. E. Henley. Thus one finds: "he was contemplat*ing*, try*ing* on a pair of boots." "The *ones* he had were a very comfortable fit." There is also a split infinitive. Moreover, Mr. Wells seems actually to have overlooked a scientific point. If the man was invisible his eyelids must have been transparent, and his eyes, without their natural shield, must speedily have become useless from simple irritation. This difficulty ought to have been got over. These things are of course trifles, but they deserve attention.

Woman, No. 405 (29 September 1897), p. 9.

R 2

APPENDIX B

HERBERT GEORGE WELLS AND HIS WORK

BY E. A. BENNETT

"The aim and the test and the justification of the scientific process is prophecy."

The prophet whose *Anticipations* have so profoundly impressed thoughtful people that no less serious a person than Mr. William Archer has proposed in a London newspaper that he should be endowed with an annual income on condition of continuing to prophesy, has hitherto somewhat suffered, in the public estimate, under the disadvantage of being wrongly labelled. It is a fact that his work is at least as diverse as that of any living prose-writer. In the seven years since he ascended into the literary firmament he has given forth "scientific romances" such as *The Time Machine, The Invisible Man, The Island of Doctor Moreau, The War of the Worlds, When the Sleeper Wakes,* and *The First Men in the Moon;* satiric fantasias, such as *The Wonderful Visit* and *The Sea Lady;* a naturalistic romance, in *The Wheels of Chance;* a realistic novel of modern life, in *Love and Mr. Lewisham;* a couple of volumes of sketches and essays; about half a hundred "strange stories," in all veins, from that of Poe to that of Guy de Maupassant; and finally the aforesaid *Anticipations,* which are as a lamp to the feet of the

twentieth century. Nevertheless, and despite all this, if
you mention the name of H. G. Wells to the man in the
street, he is fairly sure to exclaim, "Oh, yes, the disciple
of Jules Verne." Even critics who think to render the
acme of praise call him "the English Jules Verne." And
critics who wish to patronize refer to his "*pseudo-*
scientific romances."

Now, I may usefully begin to define Mr. Wells by
showing what he is not. He is not the English Jules Verne;
he does not belong to the vast Jules Verne school; and
his scientific romances are not pseudo-scientific. It con-
veniently happens that both Jules Verne and Mr. Wells
have travelled to the moon, and therefore I will come
down to particulars by contrasting the famous *From the
Earth to the Moon* and its sequel *Around the Moon*, with
Mr. Wells's *First Men in the Moon*. Jules Verne, by the
way, did not invent the moon as a place of celestial resort; Jean Baudoin, Cyrano de Bergerac, Fontenelle and
Edgar Allan Poe had been there before him. In Jules
Verne's lunar romance, the note of farcical humour is
struck at the commencement and it sounds with increasing mirth to the very end. His city of Baltimore is a
farcical city; his Yankees, Impey Barbicane and J. T.
Maston, are uproarious puppets of the vaudeville stage;
even his Frenchman, Michel Ardan, is a "type" of the
broadest. His Gun Club is magnificently farcical. You
will remember how, at the notorious mass-meeting of
thousands of savants at 21 Union Square, the president's

chair, "supported by a carved gun-carriage, was modelled upon the ponderous proportions of a thirty-two-inch mortar. It was pointed at an angle of ninety degrees, and suspended upon trunions, so that the president could balance himself upon it as upon a rocking-chair, a very agreeable fact in the hot weather"; and how the inkstand was made out of a gun, and order was kept by means of a bell that gave a "report equal to that of a revolver"; and how at the conclusion of his speech the orator, overcome with "emotion, sat down and applied himself to a huge plate of sandwiches." Jules Verne troubles but little about science. He talks with naïve and large satisfaction about "the immutable laws of mechanics," but the immutable laws of mechanics are only dragged into the story here and there to give it a fictitious sanction. We find, for instance, the secretary "rapidly tracing a few algebraical formulae upon paper, among which n^2 and x^2 frequently appeared." The immutable laws of mechanics are no longer immutable when the projectile, full of air, is opened to emit the dead dog into spatial vacuum and practically no air escapes; nor are they absolutely changeless when the rockets are fired to give impetus by their recoil; nor when a thermometer is hung out on a string to measure an interstellar frostiness of $140°$ Centigrade below zero. Moreover, Jules Verne's airy argonauts do not achieve the moon; had they done so, they could never have returned to tell the tale. They circle round what the author in a Hugoesque mood calls the Queen of

Night; and that detail alone serves to illustrate Jules Verne's propensity to shirk serious scientific problems. In saying this, my aim is, not to depreciate Jules Verne, but simply to differentiate him from Mr. Wells. *From the Earth to the Moon* and *Around the Moon* are delightful and indeed unique books. They exhibit an extraordinary gift of narrative; a free and fantastic grace of style, and a rich, broad humour which no imitator has ever approached. They are entirely delicious. But they live by their humour and verve and not at all by their illusion of reality or their dexterous handling of the immutable laws of mechanics. They never convince——nothing in them convinces, from the casting of the gun hundreds of feet long, to the returning projectile's final splash which breaks the bowsprit of the *Susquehanna*. They do not convince; they divert. When we look back upon the books, it is episodes such as Barbicana's acceptance of the wager, or the wrecking of the Baltimore theatre where a foolish manager had put on *Much Ado about Nothing*, that we recollect, not the scientific descriptions of the moon.

The great difference between Jules Verne and Mr. Wells is that the latter was trained in scientific methods of thought, while the former was not. Before Jules Verne took to romances, he wrote operatic libretti. Before Mr. Wells took to romances, he was a pupil of Huxley's at the Royal College of Science; he graduated at London University with first-class honours in science; and his first literary production, if I mistake not, was a text-book of biology. Those who prefix "pseudo" to the scientific part of Mr. Wells's novels are not the men of science. On the contrary, one may pleasantly observe the experts of *Nature*, a scientific organ of unrivalled authority, discussing the gravitational phenomena of *The First Men in the Moon*, with the aid of diagrams, and admitting that Mr. Wells has the law on his side. The qualities of *The First Men in the Moon* are fourfold. There is first the mere human psychology. We begin with two human beings, Mr. Cavor the inventor, and Mr. Bedford the narrator. They are real persons, realistically described, and whether Mr. Cavor stands abashed before the Grand Lunar, or Mr. Bedford floats alone in infinite space, neither of them once loses his individuality or ceases to act or think in a perfectly credible and convincing way. Secondly, there is the scientific machinery of the narrative, always brilliantly invented, lucidly set forth, and certainly not yet impugned by science. Thirdly, there is the graphic, picturesque side of the affair, as examples of which I may refer to the splendid sunrise on the moon, the terrible lunar night, and that really wonderful instance of close creative thought, the exposition of the air-currents through the caverns of the moon. Fourthly, and to my mind most important, there is what I must call, for lack of a better term, the philosophic quality, that quality which is fundamental in all Mr. Wells's work, and which here is principally active in the invention of the natural history and the social organization of the moon. "Naturally," says Bedford—and we should mark that "naturally," for it discloses the true bent of Mr. Wells's mind—"naturally, as living beings our interest centres far more upon the strange community of lunar insects in which Cavor was living than upon the mere physical condition of their world."

It is impossible not to perceive in Mr. Wells's powerful and sinister projection of the lunar world a deeply satiric comment upon this our earthly epoch of specialization. Among the Selenites, it will be remembered, a race distantly resembling mankind, specialization was carried to the final degree. "Every citizen knows his place. He is born to that place, and the elaborate discipline of training and education and surgery he undergoes fits him at last so completely to it that he has neither ideas nor organs for any purpose beyond it." Some Selenites were all brain, others all limbs. Some could do nothing but remember (living histories and encyclopedias); others could only carry; others could only analogize; still others could only draw. Thus Phi-oo's broken-English description of the artist: "Eat little—drink little—draw. Love draw. No other thing. Hate all who not draw like him. Angry. Hate all who draw like him better. Hate most people. Hate all who not think all world for to draw. Angry. M'm. All things mean nothing to him— only draw. He like you . . . if you understand. . . . New thing to draw. Ugly—striking. Eh?" And this more awesome and pathetic passage from Cavor's Marconi message to earth: "I came upon a number of young Selenites confined in jars from which only the fore-limbs protruded, who were being compressed to become machine-minders of a special sort. The extended 'hand' in this highly developed system of technical education is stimulated by irritants and nourished by injection, while the rest of the body is starved. . . It is quite unreasonable, I know, but such glimpses of the educational methods of these beings affected me disagreeably. I hope, however, that may pass off, and I may be able to see more of this aspect of their wonderful social order. That wretched-looking hand-tentacle sticking out of its jar seemed to have a sort of limp appeal for lost possibilities; it haunts me still, although, of course, it is really in the end a far more humane proceeding than our earthly method of leaving children to grow into human beings and then making machines of them."

Here, in the guise of romance, is a serious criticism of life, and this sober philosophic spirit decked in the picturesque colours of fantasy pervades all the latter part of the book, growing more and more impressive until it reaches its culmination in the sublime apparition of the Grand Lunar, that calm and supreme pure Intelligence who was so disturbed by Cavor's account of our incredibly ridiculous Earth that he killed the traveller, in order to prevent any organized invasion of the moon from this terrene ball of lust, bloodshed and the Absurd.

Having dissipated, I hope, the Jules Verne theory of Mr. Wells's ancestry, and incidentally examined his latest and best "scientific romance," I may proceed to a more general consideration of his work. In the year 1895, besides *The Time Machine*, which made his reputation, Mr. Wells, as if to indicate at once the various lines on which he would develop, published a volume of sketches, a volume of short stories, and that extraordinary fantastic irony, *The Wonderful Visit*, which many people regard as the most perfect and delightful thing he has yet accomplished. Touching the last first, it may be said that *The Wonderful Visit*, together with its successor in the same kind, *The Sea Lady*, stands a little apart from the main body of the author's productions. But in the record of the sojourn of the angel in the convention-ridden village, and of the mermaid in the convention-ridden seaside resort, are apparent the moral and imaginative qualities which have enabled Mr. Wells to deal so effectively with themes conceived on a much grander scale. This moral and this imaginative quality are really two sides of one gift—the gift of seeing things afresh, as though no one had ever seen them before, a gift of being able to forget all labels, preconceptions and formulae devised and invented by other people, of approaching the investigation of phenomena with senses absolutely virginal. It is the peculiar attribute of the artist; it should be, but often is not, the peculiar attribute of the moralist. Mr. Wells the artist and Mr. Wells the moralist (I scarcely know which is paramount) possess it in an abnormal degree. Once the angel arrives in the village, that village ceases to be a village and becomes a concatenation of inexplicable phenomena—inexplicable not only to the angel, but also to the good vicar who endeavours to explain them. To the angel's reiterated "Why? why? why?" there is no answer save the irrational, "Because it has always been so," "Because people have agreed that it shall be so," "Because it would never do to alter it." After the angel has perambulated the village, and especially after he has played the violin at Lady Hammergallow's party, the reader is overcome with a disconcerting and blinding vision of things as they actually are, and he sees suddenly how much of beauty and joy and sweet reasonableness humanity loses by its habit of clinging to the past instead of reaching forward to the future. The most illuminating part of the book is the vicar's long and poignant reply to the angel's remark: "This life of yours—I'm still in the dark about it. How do you begin?" I will quote briefly from the end of it:—

"And the other people here—how and why is too long a story—have made me a kind of chorus to their lives. They bring their little pink babies to me and I have to say a name and some other things over each new pink baby. And when the children have grown to be youths and maidens, they come again and are confirmed. You will understand that better later. Then before they may join in couples and have little pink babies of their own, they must come again and hear me read out of a book. They would be outcast, and no other maiden would speak to the maiden who had a little pink baby without I had read over her for twenty minutes out of my book. It's a necessary thing, as you will see, odd as it may seem to you. And afterward when they are falling to pieces, I try and persuade them of a strange world in which I scarcely believe myself, where life is altogether different from what they have had—or desire. And in the end, I bury them, and read out of my book to those who will presently follow into the unknown land. I stand at the beginning, and at the zenith, and at the setting of their lives. And on every seventh day, I who am a man myself, I who see no further than they do, talk to them of the life to come—the life of which we know nothing, if such a life there be. And slowly I drop to pieces amidst my prophesying."

"What a strange life!" said the angel.

"Yes," said the vicar, "what a strange life! But the thing that makes it strange to me is new. I had taken it as a matter of course until you came into my life."

I had taken it as a matter of course! That is precisely the attitude of which Mr. Wells's attitude is the antipodes. With him, nothing is of course, and every one who converses with him at any length finds this out first. Under all the wit, the humour, the pathos, the wayward beauty of *The Wonderful Visit* may be perceived this firm and continuous intention—to criticize the social fabric, to demand of each part of it the reason for its existence, and in default of a reply, to laugh it out of existence.

The Wheels of Chance is a quasi-satiric romance from which the supernatural element is excluded. Its hero, Mr. Hoopdriver, the draper's assistant who issued forth on a bicycle tour, fell in with a maid, stole a bicycle, and duly returned to his counter, is the best-loved of all Mr. Wells's creations. But I can merely mention the book here as the precursor of the realistic novel, *Love and Mr. Lewisham*, the only novel, in the usual meaning of the term, which Mr. Wells has yet written, but which is surely to be followed by others. In it we have the history of a student of science with lofty ideals who got into the toils of that blind force of nature which we call love, and was, in a worldly sense, thereby utterly ruined. The sayings of Mr. Chaffery, that audacious and unmoral spirit who saw things as they are and gained a livelihood by deceiving the fools who wanted to be deceived, are the memorable utterances in the book. Here, for example, is Mr. Chaffery's recipe for a happy life: "In youth, exercise and learning; in adolescence, ambition, and in early manhood, love—no footlight passion. Then marriage, young and decent, and then children and stout honest work for themselves and for the State in which they live; a life of self-devotion, indeed, and for sunset a decent pride— that is the happy life . . . the life Natural Selection has been shaping for man since life began. So a man may go happy from the cradle to the grave—at least passably happy. And to do this needs just three things—a sound body, a sound intelligence, and a sound will. . . A sound will. No other happiness endures. And when all men are wise, all men will seek that life. Fame! Wealth! Art! The Red Indians worship lunatics, and we are still by way of respecting the milder sorts. But I say that all men who do not lead that happy life are knaves and fools." So that only in the worldly sense was Lewisham ruined. At the end of the book, as he stands staring through the window, thinking of his career perforce abandoned and of the prospect of immediate fatherhood ("the most important career in the world"), his feelings are symbolized for us in an image of really exquisite beauty—"The dwindling light gathered itself together and became a star."

Here, therefore, even in the realistic novel of modern matter-of-fact, we are not allowed to get away from the scientific principles that man is a part of nature, that he is a creature of imperious natural forces, that he is only one link in the chain of eternal evolution.

In the "scientific romances," to which we may now at last come, the principle of evolution and a conception of "man's place in nature" are Mr. Wells's great basic facts.

In his lecture on "The Discovery of the Future," delivered at the Royal Institution on January 24th last, Mr. Wells contrasted two divergent types of mind, distinguishable "chiefly by their attitude toward time and more particularly by the relative importance they attach, and the relative amount of importance they give, to the future of things." The first type of mind, he continued, interprets the things of the present, and gives value to this and denies it to that, entirely with relation to the past. The second type is constructive in habit; it interprets the things of the present, and gives value to this or that, entirely in relation to things designed or foreseen. "While from that former point of view our life is simply to reap the consequences of the past, from this our life is to prepare the future." And he said further: "The former type one might speak of as the legal or submissive type of mind, because the business, the practice and the training of a lawyer dispose him toward it; he of all men must most constantly refer to the law made, the right established, the precedent set, and most consistently ignore or condemn the thing that is only seeking to establish itself. The latter type of mind I might for contrast call the legislative, organizing or masterful type, because it is perpetually attacking and altering the established order of things, perpetually falling away from respect for what the past has given us. *It sees the world as one great workshop and the present is no more than material for the future, for the thing that is destined yet to be.* It is in the active mood of thought, while the former is in the passive; it is the mind of youth, it is the mind more manifest among the Western nations; while the former is the mind of age— the mind of the Oriental. Things have been, says the legal mind, and so we are here. *And the creative mind says, we are here because things have yet to be.*"

The sentences which I have italicized contain the key to Mr. Wells's philosophy of life. He has no use for precedents and conventions. The past may survive only so long as it can pass the tests of reason. The present must look, never back at death, but always forward toward life. Among all Mr. Wells's tales I remember but one, "A Story of the Stone Age," which deals with the past. It is the future, it is evolution, it is innovation, which he preaches and will always preach.

He said in that same lecture: "The essential thing in the scientific process is not the collection of facts, but the analysis of facts; facts are the raw material not the substance of science; the aim and the test and the justification of the scientific process is not a marketable conjuring-trick, but prophecy. Until a scientific theory yields confident forecasts it is unsound and tentative; it is mere theorizing." So science is, ultimately, prophecy—something to help us to shape our ends. And Mr. Wells is a man of science in order, first and foremost, that he may be a prophet and map out the path so that humanity shall avoid détours. And prophecy is really what he has always been at when he has touched science. He may juggle with our ideas of time and space, as in *The Time Machine*, "The Plattner Story," "The Crystal Egg," and "The Accelerator"; he may startle or shock us by the artistic presentation of a scientific "conjuring-trick," as in *The Invisible Man* and *The Island of Doctor Moreau*; he may awe us by sheer force of an original imaginative conception, as in "The Star," "Under the Knife," and "The Man Who Could Work Miracles." But his real, preferred business has been to prophesy, to peer into the future. In *The Time Machine*, the Time-Traveller goes forward, not into "the dark backward and abysm." Mr. Wells's fancy was youthful in those days, and the Time-Traveller journeyed through a million years or so; he saw a grim and terrible vision of the evolution of the "submerged tenth" and the "upper classes," a world murderously divided against itself, a world in which it seemed that the aspirations and sacrifices and sufferings of mankind had come to nothing at all, had ended in utter moral disaster. He went further and witnessed the more fatigued revolution of a planet occupied by monsters round a sun dying of radiation. He watched what was the apparent final stultification of a Supreme Purpose. Then he came back and with a sublime and justifiable audacity remarked to his friends: "No. I cannot expect you to believe it. Take it as a lie— or a prophecy. Say I dreamed it in the workshop. Consider I have been speculating upon the destinies of our race, until I have hatched this fiction. Treat my assertion of its truth as a mere stroke of art to enhance its interest. And taking it as a story, what do you think of it?"

The War of the Worlds was not a prophecy, but it was in the nature of a prophecy, a speculative, warning criticism, so far as it described an organization of intelligent beings more advanced than our own. And the same is to be said of *The First Men in the Moon*. In *When the*

Sleeper Wakes and "A Story of the Days to Come," Mr. Wells returned to prophecy in fiction. But it was a much quieter, soberer, humbler, and an infinitely more useful prophecy than that of *The Time Machine*. Instead of dealing with thousands and millions of years, he dealt with a century or so. And in *Anticipations of the Reaction of Mechanical and Scientific Progress upon Human Life and Thought*, he has abandoned the garb of fiction, and he definitely stands forth naked and unashamed as a prophet of the real. My personal opinion is that he will work still more strenuously in this field, and that in the course of a few years, passing down toward the present through a series of futures less and less remote (he has already retreated from thirty millions years hence to a hundred hence), he may develop, still flying all his flags of imagination, fancy, humour, satire and irony, into an actual, prevalent political force. His strongest points are his clear vision and his intellectual honesty and courage; his weakest point is his instinctive antipathy to any static condition.

And his forecast of the more immediate future, his creed? You may see it set out with surprisingly close texture of detail in *Anticipations*; and in a forthcoming series of essays, possibly more boldly creative in character than *Anticipations*, the instant means to the Great End may be shadowed forth as they present themselves to his mind. Suffice it to say here that Mr. Wells firmly believes in universal peace and in the high destiny of nature, *The*

Time Machine of seven years ago notwithstanding. "It it not difficult," he has said, "to collect reasons for supposing that humanity will be definitely and consciously organizing itself as a great world-state—a great world-state that will purge itself from much that is mean, much that is bestial, and much that makes for individual dullness and dreariness, greyness and wretchedness in the world of to-day."

"And finally," he added, "there is the reasonable certainty that . . . this earth of ours, tideless and slow-moving, will be dead and frozen, and all that has lived upon it will be frozen out and done with. There surely man must end. That of all such nightmares is the most insistently convincing. And yet one doesn't believe it. At least I do not. And I do not believe in these things because I have come to believe in certain other things—in the coherency and purpose in the world and in the greatness of human destiny. Worlds may freeze and suns may perish, but there stirs something within us now that can never die again."

And this by way of postscript: "The most persistently fascinating and the most insoluble question in the whole world is—what is to come *after* man?"

The *Cosmopolitan Magazine*, XXXIII (August 1902), 465–471.

APPENDIX C

BENNETT'S LETTER ON WELLS'S BEHALF TO THE AUTHORS' SOCIETY

In the following letter Bennett is taking Wells's side in Wells's dispute with the Incorporated Society of Authors, Playwrights and Composers and a former collaborator, Hugh P. Vowels. Wells had planned in 1928 a third and final work, *The Science of Work and Wealth*, in his project to present a popular statement of the current knowledge of man, the first two works being *The Outline of History* and *The Science of Life*. He chose as collaborators for this third work Edward Cressy (later C. H. Creasy), an experienced writer on industrial subjects, and Hugh P. Vowels, a mechanical engineer and a fervent disciple of Wells since 1909. According to Wells, "I did not so much want equals . . . as intelligent, industrious fags." The first book of the new work was to be entitled *Conquest of Power*.

By August 1929, however, Wells had developed deep reservations concerning Vowels and postponed the project indefinitely. Vowels took his grievance to the Society of Authors and, amid a stormy correspondence, a writ was issued against Wells for breach of contract. The writ was later withdrawn, and the dispute was placed in the hands of an arbitrator, Sir Donald Maclean. Vowels was awarded £1500 in damages in lieu of the £6000 share in royalties that Wells had originally promised him. (Actually Vowels was awarded only £700, since Wells had already advanced him, during their brief collaboration, £800.) On the intervention and counsel of G. B. Shaw, Wells grudgingly accepted the settlement.

Wells presents his side of the dispute in a privately printed pamphlet, *The Problem of the Troublesome Collaborator, Printed for circulation among the members of the Society of Authors for their information and not for publication*, 1930, in which he vehemently defends his actions, and excoriates Vowels and G. Herbert Thring, Secretary of the Authors' Society. His reluctant compromise is presented in another privately printed pamphlet, *Settlement of the Trouble Between Mr. Thring and Mr. Wells, A Footnote to the Problem of the Troublesome Collaborator, Printed for private circulation only among those who received the previous pamphlet*, 1930.

It should be noted, however, that before he composed the staunch defence of Wells that follows, Bennett wrote: "I found in the post a long, typewritten statement by H. G. W. about his difficulties with his collaborators and the Authors' Society in his projected work, *The Science of Work and Wealth*. I read it all in my bedroom before going to bed. It took twenty-six minutes' full reading. It makes a rather sad *exposé*, by H. G. himself, of his violent demeanour in writing business letters when he gets cross, ill or worried." (Pound, p. 355.)

10 *March* 1930

DEAR LORD GORELL,

In reference to your circular letter of the 4th March with its personal postscript, I have now studied this dossier with some care, and I should like to make a few observations, not upon the merits of the case, but upon the Society's handling of the case as revealed by the correspondence.

1. In his letter to Mr. Wells of the 8th November the Secretary says that the practice of the Society, when consulted by one member, A, about a dispute with another member, B, is first of all to take counsel's opinion. This procedure seems to me to be rather strange. I should have thought the first step would be to make some effort to bring the disputants together, or at least to ask B for *his* version of the dispute.

Why should the Society incur the expense attendant upon instructing a solicitor to instruct counsel before a peaceful settlement has been even attempted? Is this the best way of promoting friendliness? And is the fighting fund of the Society so ample that it can afford to incur legal costs which in the sequel may prove to have been unnecessary? If the practice of the Society is indeed what the secretary says it is, then I venture the view that the sooner it is altered the better.

2. Mr. Wells asked again and again for some particulars of the "nature and terms" of the alleged contract on

which the plaintiff was basing his claim. Apparently he never received an answer. Indeed the fixed intention of the Society seems to have been to refuse all information to Mr. Wells, for the latter was unable to obtain from the Secretary the most ordinary particulars of membership of the Committee of Management until he consulted a solicitor who insisted on delivery of those particulars.

3. It would appear that the alleged contract between the parties was partly in writing and partly verbal. As Counsel had only had the plaintiff's account of the verbal part of the contract, he must obviously have based his opinion on an *ex parte* statement. And on the strength of an opinion so based the Society advised the plaintiff to institute proceedings.

4. A Writ was issued and a statement of claim delivered; the action is pursuing the ordinary course. Yet in your circular letter of the 4th you say that the Committee are giving the dispute "their most earnest attention in the hope of bringing it to a just conclusion." Surely this most earnest attention on the part of the Committee ought to have been bestowed on the affair before and not after the issue of the Writ?

5. In your circular letter of the 4th you say: "Mr. Thring has throughout acted strictly in accordance with directions received from the Committee." Have you overlooked the third paragraph in the secretary's letter of the 4th November to Mr. Wells, in which he specifically states that the suggestion it contains is made without the

authority of the Committee? This unauthorized suggestion might have been accepted as a benevolent attempt to secure peace were it not the fact that the suggestion itself partially begs the question. The secretary speaks of "the extent of your responsibility." What right had the secretary to assume that there was any responsibility, having regard to all the circumstances detailed by Mr. Wells in his letter to Mr. Thring of November 9th?

To my mind the secretary's attitude throughout shows a marked *parti pris* in favour of the plaintiff. *If* it be argued that the secretary felt aggrieved by the tone of some of Mr. Wells's letters to him, I would say that one of the chief duties of the secretary in a dispute between members is to keep his feelings entirely in abeyance. I do not say that the secretary did not keep his own feelings in abeyance. I do not say that as a man he had not some ground for irritation. But I do say that as a secretary he was not entitled to be swayed in the slightest degree by the tone of the correspondence. I hope that he was not so swayed. And I say further that Mr. Wells's letters were written under what I myself would consider extreme provocation and when he was physically indisposed. Mr. Wells might be excused for thinking that the secretary was treating him not as a member of the Society but as some dubious publisher should be treated.

6. Personally I cannot see that Mr. Wells in the correspondence suggested that the secretary should retire "without pension of any kind." Rather he suggested that

the secretary ought not to be appointed "Consulting Secretary." I share this view. I would not, however, for one moment imply that the secretary has not loyally served the Society to the best of his ability during a long term of years. I think he has.

7. Finally we have the spectacle of the Society's official solicitors, their costs no doubt guaranteed by the Society, acting in a suit precipitately brought on evidence to some extent *ex parte*, against a member of the Society. This spectacle seems to me to be offensive in a high degree, and repugnant to the amenities of the Society. For myself I most strongly object to any part of any subscriptions of my own being applied to the upholding of such an action. And if the action is persisted in I shall be compelled to consider my position not only as a member of the Council but as a member of the Society. I am not alone in this attitude.

I need not assure you, my dear Chairman, that nothing I have said is applicable personally to yourself, of whose unselfish work on behalf of the Society I have the highest appreciation.

Yours sincerely

ARNOLD BENNETT

INDEX